Copyright © 2023 by Kyndall Bennett - All rights reserved.

The content contained within this book may not be reproduced, duplicated or transmitted without direct written permission from the author or the publisher. Under no circumstances will any blame or legal responsibility be held against the publisher, or author, for any damages, reparation, or monetary loss due to the information contained within this book. Either directly or indirectly. You are responsible for your own choices, actions, and results.

Legal Notice:

This book is copyright protected. This book is only for personal use. You cannot amend, distribute, sell, use, quote or paraphrase any part, or the content within this book, without the consent of the author or publisher.

Disclaimer Notice:

Please note the information contained within this document is for educational and entertainment purposes only. All effort has been executed to present accurate, up to date, and reliable, complete information. No warranties of any kind are declared or implied. Readers acknowledge that the author is not engaging in the rendering of legal, financial, medical or professional advice. The content within this book has been derived from various sources. Please consult a licensed professional before attempting any techniques outlined in this book.

By reading this document, the reader agrees that under no circumstances is the author responsible for any losses, direct or indirect, which are incurred as a result of the use of the information contained within this document, including, but not limited to, — errors, omissions, or inaccuracies.

Additional Credit:

Cover design - Carolina Soares

Research - Publishing Services

Writing - Widhi Way

Editing - AJ Kearney

Visit the blog at KyrabeStories.com for more helpful resources.

Complete the Series

Grab a copy of *She's Meant to Lead* to complement what you are about to learn within *She's Meant to Speak*! The books can be read in any order that you see fit for your goals.

Contents

Introduction   1

1. Why We Don't Speak   4
    Challenges Women Face With Communication in the Workplace
    Why Do Women Struggle to Assert Themselves in Leadership Positions?
    Breaking Through the External Barriers
    The Reality of Being a Leader from a Minority Group
    What Is the Glass Cliff Phenomenon?
    What Makes an Excellent Communicator?
    Are You a Good Communicator?

2. Body Language and Nonverbal Cues   20
    The Significance of Body Language
    Getting Better at Understanding Facial Expressions
    What Your Body Is Telling Others
    Other Vocal, Nonverbal, and Habitual Cues That Impact Communication
    Reading the Whole Room

3. Taking Your Voice to the Next Level   36
    What Is Your Communication Style?
    There Is No Such Thing as "Winging It"

      Using Your Words Wisely
      What Message Does Your Appearance Convey?

4. Communication in the Digital World   54
      Pros and Cons of the Digital Workplace
      A Guide to Choosing Communication and Project Management Software
      How to Improve Your Written Communication
      Using Instant Messaging to Your Advantage
      What You Need to Remember About Video Conferencing
      Overcoming Communication Barriers

The Value of Support   69

5. The Part of Communication That Many Leaders Forget   71
      What Does It Mean to Be an Active Listener?
      Steps to Being a Better Listener
      What Happens When a Team Has an Empathetic Leader?
      How to Be an Empathetic Yet Strong Female Leader
      Becoming a Good Leader

6. Networking Like a Queen Bee   85
      The Difference Between Mentors and Sponsors
      How to Succeed at Networking Events
      Conversation Topics That Will Make You Stand Out
      Ending Conversations Gracefully
      Setting the Example and Creating Networking Events
      The Best Places to Network

7. Assertive Communication and Conflict Resolution   100
    How Can Women Master the Communication Balance?
    Setting Boundaries Within Your Team
    The Art of Delegating Without Nagging
    Giving and Receiving Constructive Criticism
    How to Resolve Conflicts Collaboratively
    Negotiating What You Deserve
    Examples of Passive, Aggressive, and Assertive Communication

8. Dealing With Racism, Sexism, and Other Toxic Behaviors   115
    What Are Microaggressions?
    Other Examples of Toxic Behavior
    How to Deal With Toxic Behavior in the Workplace
    Creating a Positive Workplace Culture
    Toxic Work Culture Checklist

Conclusion   128

References   130

Acknowledgements   142

Introduction

Communication is the sister of leadership. –John Adair

The decision to write this book was made when I was speaking to a friend of mine. We'll call her Stephanie. She had just been promoted to a managerial position in her division. She is well-qualified, a hard worker, and has performed her best to get to this position. She told me that when she needed to attend her first managerial meeting, she was relieved to know that there was another woman who had the same position as her. As they were to be only two women there, she was confident that they would support each other when in need. In this meeting, Stephanie was determined to make her voice heard, even when she was surrounded by men. But when the time came for her presentation, she froze up the second someone asked a question and all eyes were suddenly on her. She knew that the answer was right there on the tip of her tongue, but imposter syndrome kicked in. She felt down and thought that she didn't deserve to have her position at work. What made it worse was that the other female manager had rolled her eyes rather than throwing a supportive look.

Stephanie is definitely not the only woman who has gone through this experience. Sometimes, you might feel that you don't deserve to be given a promotion—that there are other more qualified candidates for the position. Other times, it can feel like a struggle to even voice an opinion in the face of regular dismissal from male colleagues. Sadly, there are still a lot of stereotypes about women in the workplace. Women are often painted as unqualified for their jobs purely because they are female. This stereotype may lead many women to have imposter syndrome. We are fed these lies our whole lives, and this makes us believe that we cannot make any mistakes if we want to be recognized. This form of stigma means that women must fight so hard to get into leadership positions, but then, they also have to struggle much harder to prove they deserve them, and there is absolutely no room for error. If a man loses his temper, people jump into action to help him and excuse his behavior. If a woman does so much as raise her voice, she is likely to be labeled "hormonal," told she can't cope with the stress, and hearing people say that she is not qualified.

Now is the time for us to take action. If we do not stand up and make a change, future generations will only continue to struggle. Our race or gender should never impact our experiences in the workplace. We ought to be judged solely on our skills and ability to perform our professional duties. Yet, nevertheless, women—and in particular, women of color—are routinely dismissed according to prejudicial stereotypes. One of the most powerful ways that we can disrupt this pattern of discrimination is to speak up, and learning to communicate effectively ensures that when we do speak up, we will be heard, respected, and capable of prompting much-needed change.

Are you looking to improve your communication skills and unlock your voice? You have come to the right place. This book provides you with insights on how to more effectively communicate with anyone in the workplace, whether it is your team members or other managers. Through the application of these skills, you can also increase the effectiveness of your team in the process. More importantly, you will improve office culture and set a positive example for other female leaders around you.

Let's take an example of a successful female leader: Elizabeth Warren, a well-known U.S. Senator. Since she was a young girl in the 1950s, she had wanted to be a working woman, but her mother was worried that Warren would never find a husband if she decided to work. However, she didn't listen to her mother and went to Georgetown University with a full scholarship because she was excellent at debating. Although she dropped out to get married, she returned to college to study law at Rutgers. She eventually graduated, while pregnant with her second baby. At the time, it was difficult for her to find a job because not many firms hired female lawyers. This was until she received help in landing a teaching position at Rutgers from one of her professors. Her teaching career quickly expanded after that, and she got jobs at different universities.

Warren's journey to becoming a senator was not easy. She has said that if women want to be in power, they need to fight for it when given a chance. No one was willing to give up their position in power to make space at the table for female leaders, so Warren struggled to get a spot there. In order to achieve success, she had to learn how to communicate effectively and express her opinions, even among intimidating men. Women are often considered "too weak" to become leaders, but Warren proved this stereotype wrong.

Have you dreamed of being a successful leader like Elizabeth Warren? Every one of us can do it too. You can learn how to communicate effectively by following the guidance laid out within the pages of this book. Imagine yourself being a leader where your team respects and listens to you: No one will look down on you anymore if you understand how to assert yourself in your position at the office. These are the things that you may gain by reading this book.

Are you ready to improve your communication skills at the workplace? Let's explore and learn the strategies that will help.

1
Why We Don't Speak

"I raise up my voice – not so I can shout, but so that those without a voice can be heard...we cannot succeed when half of us are held back." – Malala Yousafzai

We have seen time and time again that women surpass their male counterparts in the majority of leadership capabilities—even communication, surprisingly. Yet, the stereotypes and biases surrounding women in the workplace, and more so in leadership positions, have been around for centuries and are incredibly hard to change. So, we must ask why—even with all the science and research behind us—is it still so hard to be seen as even close to an equal?

Challenges Women Face With Communication in the Workplace

According to Ragini Verma, a researcher of radiology at the University of Pennsylvania, women's brains appear to have more powerful connections between their intuitive and logical areas when given challenging tasks. This means that women may use various parts of the brain when they need to do especially difficult tasks, whereas men might use a single part of their brains excessively (Khazan, 2013). Additionally, women's brains receive a greater flow of blood when accessing areas devoted to memory, language, and emotion, making these parts more highly active than those of their male counterparts (Valenzuela, 2022). Because of this, men may have a tendency to see problems and jump to solve them quickly, but women may be more likely to mix logic and instinct when addressing a problem which makes them better at communicating complex concepts. Although women are biologically better at communicating, there are also some challenges that they have to face in a work setting. The following are a few of these challenges.

Taking Credit for Their Accomplishments

Many women refuse to advocate for themselves and their accomplishments. Of course, there is a time to be humble, but that is generally not at your workplace. Nevertheless, many of us are socialized to believe that speaking up for ourselves equates to "cockiness," "bossiness," or worse. But in order to gain respect in the workplace, we must first acknowledge, respect, and praise our own achievements: Own it if you contributed a lot to a project. You might want to dismiss your accomplishments as the result of teamwork, but it is not wrong to take credit for the good things that you do. Men typically like to take credit and are not hesitant to state their accomplishments in a way that makes it evident who got the desired outcomes, so why would we hold ourselves to completely different standards of behavior? When you get compliments for your work, try not to say that it was nothing; you deserve to recognize this success saying that you have worked hard to achieve it.

Acknowledging your value and communicating it to your supervisor and team is essential. This is because you have special qualities and skill sets that helped you to get your position in the first place. The first move to improving your sense of self is speaking out and advocating for yourself whenever you achieve something.

Ruminating and Taking Things Personally

Women are more inclined to take things personally when something uncomfortable or unpleasant occurs at work. We don't usually think of our work as just a business. We treat our jobs very seriously because they are important and meaningful pursuits. However, some women approach regular work circumstances with a little bit too much personal drive and enthusiasm, which can lead them to get off track. When we do this, we waste our valuable time worrying or concentrating on the individual who offended us instead of solving the problem. It is admirable to care deeply about your professional and social success, but when this devolves into rumination or people-pleasing tendencies, it becomes counterproductive and needs to be challenged. We need to work to critically assess what is happening in a situation before reacting so that we can respond effectively. If we simply act based on our emotions, we put our ability to make wise decisions and think from a more level-headed, leadership-focused perspective at risk.

Challenging Authority

It can be difficult for anyone to stand up and confront those in positions of power and authority, but women tend to find it particularly hard to do so. More often than not, we are undervalued in the workplace. We frequently get cut off and talked over in conversations by our male counterparts. Moreover, we frequently experience anxiety when we are in positions of leadership since we are often required to demonstrate our skill set more. This is compounded by the fact that we often find ourselves in a double bind when it comes to expressing femininity in the workplace: While stereotypically feminine communication traits—such as being soft-spoken, gently approaching topics, and seeking affirmative reactions with questions like, "you know?"—are often seen as signs of "weakness," people also find it unsettling when women act in assertive, confident ways that are typically associated with men so that we can be taken seriously. As a result, when we act in this manner, we are frequently criticized as being obnoxious, confrontational, or harsh. This then challenges our ability to lead with confidence.

Women are really caught in a dilemma. If we are not confident, no one will take us seriously and we will never advance our careers. Yet, we also can't risk gaining a reputation for being overly domineering. It is quite difficult for us to walk this thin line between being taken seriously and being considered off-putting for being confident in doing our jobs. Then, how do women challenge authority more? By combining effective assertive communication skills with a careful examination of the environment and culture at your workplace, you *can* go beyond surviving and even flourish there.

Using Confident Body Language

Meetings at the office can be intimidating. If you feel too anxious to voice your thoughts in these situations, using confident body language can be a much more accessible place to start improving your communication skills. Ensuring that you stand or sit up straight throughout the meetings will project confidence; keeping a straight posture in the workplace, counterintuitively, allows you to look more relaxed because slouching is a typical sign of anxiety and stress. Similarly, fidgeting can cause you to appear anxious, or worse, bored, and thus, it should be avoided where possible. If you get the chance to speak at the meeting, try not to make any nervous gestures that could distract others from the things you say. Prior to the meeting, it can be helpful to practice power poses by standing with your legs wide apart, putting your hands on your waist, and taking deep breaths. You may even try this in the restroom before entering the meeting room.

Finding Mentors

Women are underrepresented in the top positions of their companies, and one major factor in this is that they are not given the important projects that are necessary to advance. This is frequently caused by a lack of strong mentors who demand and guarantee that they receive higher positions. Additionally, many women may not even be aware about the importance of seeking these mentors in the first place. Men are more inherently inclined than women to obtain sponsors or seek the guidance of those within the company who are in a position to encourage their progress and advancement (Caprino, 2012).

In a mentorship, senior and powerful individuals in a company utilize their personal influence to promote, support, and put a less experienced person in an important position (Ibarra, 2019). Your success and career advancement in a company depend on obtaining a mentor who will be able to sponsor and lift you. Your sponsor is someone who has the influence to assist you to advance and get you promoted to better positions.

Negotiating to Get What They Deserve
As women, many of us have a tendency to underestimate ourselves, and we even sometimes suppress our confidence to avoid coming out as overly demanding. We particularly underestimate our ability to earn a high salary in male-dominated fields. Women who feel undervalued have an increased tolerance for poverty and are willing to work for pennies in order to make enough to survive. This is why more of us need to stand up for ourselves and negotiate better pay at our workplace.

In any industry, we should know how to effectively negotiate and talk about improvement requests, from negotiating for raises to conveying a necessary boost in performance. By knowing how to negotiate better, you will be treated with respect by your colleagues and supervisors, particularly when attending meetings with clients because you know how to get better deals.

Why Do Women Struggle to Assert Themselves in Leadership Positions?

Women in leadership positions deal with more problems and barriers in the workplace than their male peers. So, what should you do to overcome these challenges as a driven female leader? Many people believe that having more female leaders will make their workplace better. However, it can be difficult for women in leadership roles to confront discriminatory bias and high expectations. Being a female leader is certainly more difficult, but women can work to overcome these obstacles.

Communication Challenges

One of the toughest obstacles that female leaders have to face is expressing their ideas in an environment dominated by men. When a woman speaks in front of some men and offers a solution to an issue, she often realizes that nobody is paying attention, and her suggestion ends up being ignored. Yet, frequently, a short while later, a man will make the very same suggestion, and suddenly, the group of men agrees. This all too common occurrence demonstrates that a man will be taken more seriously just because he is a man. When working at a company with this kind of culture, women may feel discouraged from voicing their thoughts and would rather keep ideas to themselves so that they do not get humiliated in a male-dominated meeting.

When a woman puts forward an idea timidly with filler words like "um," or "well" and a questioning intonation, the participants of the meeting will not fully follow along with the suggestion. Many may even pity her attempt to speak at all.

For the other women in the room—particularly those who have experienced more significant harassment based on the negative stereotypes surrounding women not being adept in these environments—this can trigger passive aggression toward this woman who is still learning and developing these skills, believing she is "setting women back" in moments like these. When a woman's voice is regularly used in a timid manner, it will be ignored or devalued and she will start to question her ideas and stop sharing, in turn causing others to stop waiting for her contribution. In extreme cases, some women become overly aggressive in the hope of being heard.

These things are not advantageous to you or your company. When no one listens to you, you will feel less appreciated and think others devalue your worth. If you have ever struggled to be heard, you can certainly relate to the anger and fear caused by this specific issue. You might even ask yourself if you deserve your job at all.

However, you need to keep going. You can close the communication gap and make sure that your opinion is heard, acknowledged, and respected by learning how to overcome these challenges. Recognizing the additional communication obstacles you face is the first step in overcoming them. You have to do more to be heard as a female leader. Some key steps to overcoming communication challenges include the following:

- **Quit worrying and begin trusting:**
    - You should start believing in yourself because your opinions are just as valuable as anyone else's. You lose control if you spend too much time thinking about what other people think. You need to embrace your abilities and express your ideas.

- **Point out double standards:**
    - When a man, or even another woman, interrupts or begins to talk over you, you need to stand up

for yourself and tell him that you are still speaking. You can then emphasize again the importance of your ideas. Despite feeling angry and frustrated, it is better if you can clearly call out these inconsistencies without shouting or fighting.

- Become accustomed to self-promotion:
    - Self-promotion is typically difficult for women. Women tend to find it easier to promote those close to them rather than themselves. You need to be more comfortable sharing your opinions so that more individuals can hear about your skills and accomplishments. Although it will be very difficult in the start, you will get accustomed to it as you practice.

Breaking Through the External Barriers

Even though there are more opportunities for women nowadays, we still have trouble achieving and getting leadership positions because of discrimination. Other than communication challenges, we have to also face various barriers in the workplace. When communication is improved, these challenges are more capable for us to overcome.

The Gender Pay Gap

In the last 20 years, the gender pay gap in the US continues to be relatively constant. According to a recent Pew Research Center assessment of the median hourly wages of both full-time and part-time workers in 2022, on average, women only earned 82% of what men made (Aragao, 2023). This percentage dips even further for many BIPOC women facing the intersection of sexism and racism. Nowadays, women have improved their representation in male-dominated, higher-paying jobs, but they also still dominate a lot of low-paying jobs. In order to solve unequal pay, companies must allow women to hold positions of leadership, and women must voice their salary expectations. If we ask for little, that is what we shall receive.

Conflicting Expectations

Even though it may seem unfair, female leaders generally face higher expectations. Women in leadership positions must balance the conflicting expectations of their societal and professional roles. In society, women are usually expected to be kind, show empathy, and nurture. However, some expectations of leadership roles expect the one in the position to possess more authoritative traits like assertiveness, risk-taking, and confidence. Women leaders frequently find themselves in difficult positions due to these conflicting demands.

Unconscious Bias

Unconscious bias is the implicit forms of discrimination or stereotyping that we unintentionally act on. In relation to gender roles in the workplace, this could be anything from having unintentional thoughts about women's abilities to following gender stereotypes. Bias can also appear as an expectation for women to behave and talk in specific ways. In the workplace, unconscious biases against female employees are extremely harmful and can come from their boss, managers, and colleagues.

Gender-Based Violence and Sexual Harassment

Violence against a person that is motivated by their gender is referred to as gender-based violence, and its roots are in damaging standards and abuses of power (Lestari et al., 2019). This definition covers all gender-based types of violence against women, including sexual harassment. Sadly, this remains a serious issue to this day. Even female leaders still have to deal with harassment. According to estimates, 85% of all female workers have faced sexual harassment at work; the percentage is probably even higher for women who hold managerial and leadership positions (Botwin, 2022).

Additional Obstacles Toward Career Development

Frustratingly within male-dominated workplaces, women are less likely to be chosen for promotions or even opportunities to partake in continuous professional development. Opportunities either are not communicated properly or favor men more frequently to participate. Only a small number of companies can be named as setting best practices for developing cultures where women can thrive. Additionally, we as female leaders must take the initiative to also support the advancement of young women by connecting to, funding, and encouraging them.

The Reality of Being a Leader from a Minority Group

Those in minority groups experience more sexism as well as racism. What's more, there are even fewer mentors and sponsors to help them advance, fewer opportunities, and more challenges in their way. Moreover, they have to face more questions about their appropriateness for the leadership role. Many even feel they have to be someone they are not in order to fit in.

The impacts of discrimination increase even further when a woman of color is a member of other marginalized communities—for instance, if she is trans or Muslim. The path to becoming a leader for these women is unclear, in part due to an absence of role models and sponsors that they can relate to and can support them in reaching their goals. They also have less exposure to powerful connections, making it more difficult for them to envision a path to reach leadership roles in their companies. In short, marginalization can often be a self-sustaining vicious cycle until it is challenged.

Minority groups have insufficient guides that can lead them to their own successes. They do not get enough mentorship from successful leaders that are willing to help them. Their networks often only consist of their coworkers who have not become leaders and their own marginalized communities. But everything is possible if minority people in power lend a hand to assist their people to rise up to better positions in their companies and if those of us who do not face such marginalization commit to dismantling our unconscious biases and uplifting those who do, rather than attempting to "speak for them."

What Is the Glass Cliff Phenomenon?

We all have heard of the metaphorical glass ceiling that prevents certain people from gaining leadership roles, but over the last decade, there has been extensive research into the *glass cliff* phenomenon, where women and members of minority groups are given leadership roles that are risky—whether because a company is doing badly or in political situations that are doomed to fail, such as in the case of Teresa May and Brexit.

The glass cliff phenomenon happens in various industries, such as tech, politics, and education. It discusses the common tendency for women to be promoted into difficult circumstances that have very a low chance to be resolved. This increases the likelihood that their performance may suffer in the process. The metaphor of the glass cliff refers to how women in these circumstances run the risk of falling off a cliff (Kagan, 2022).

Let's see an example of this phenomenon: After losing a big amount of its market share in 2012, Yahoo named Marissa Mayer as its new CEO. She made a brave attempt to save Yahoo even though it was already in big trouble. Having failed to better the company, Mayer stepped down from her position after five years following much criticism. Many people condemned her for not being able to turn things around for the company, even though she was given an impossible task.

By doing this, a company can improve its public image by scapegoating a stereotypically "weak" individual rather than being forced to take accountability as an entire entity. If the woman does not succeed, the company will paint a bad image of her and then feel entitled to hire a man in her stead. If she becomes successful, the company will take credit for choosing the best candidate in solving the problem. When offered this kind of position, women have a hard time declining it despite the risk since leadership positions are so rarely given to them.

What Makes an Excellent Communicator?

Almost every leadership role will require excellent communication skills. It's not just our ability to get a message across with accuracy and clarity without waffling on; it's also about the ability to actively listen and respond so that people know you are listening. It is about your nonverbal communication matching the words you use so that mixed messages are not sent. Moreover, it is about respect.

It is often overlooked that in order to become an excellent communicator, you need to also be good at listening. When listening to someone talking, you are paying attention to what they are saying and asking questions to seek clarity and better understanding. Without you practicing active listening, your team members will suffer because they won't feel that you respect them and will think that you ignore them. You need to practice active listening to be a good communicator. This means that you have to give your undivided attention and truly take in what they are saying. Simply hearing what they say while formulating your own responses is not *actually* listening.

Another crucial aspect of effective communication is demonstrating respect for the person you are having a conversation with. Even if you disagree with their opinions, it is still crucial to demonstrate that you pay attention to and comprehend the things they say before presenting your own arguments. When talking to someone in person, you can show respect by using a steady tone of voice and smiling rather than being rude or demanding.

Uttering words is only one aspect of communication; another important thing is how you deliver them. Key components of communication include proper body language, facial expressions, and eye contact. Improper body language will result in incorrectly interpreted communication. The next time someone tries to communicate with you, try to adopt open, relaxed body language so that they can feel heard during the discussion.

Clarity and accuracy are also necessary to become an excellent communicator. This means that instead of talking vaguely without reaching any point, you need to go straight to the point. If you have a tendency to ramble on, you can prepare your points ahead of time so that you do not stray away from the points you want to communicate.

Are You a Good Communicator?

How good do you think you are at communicating? If you wish to know, you can answer these self-assessment questions. These questions can help you understand your communication skills more. You can rate your agreement with the statements below on a scale from one to five—one being not at all; five being always—and calculate the overall score for self-reflection to understand where there is room for improvement.

Statements	Scale				
	1	2	3	4	5
Prior to conversing with someone, I prepare what points I have to tell them and the most effective ways to communicate with them.					
I make an effort to foresee and anticipate potential misunderstandings, and I take care of them right away.					
I provide as much context and explanation as possible when I write something to ensure that my point is conveyed well.					
When I'm in a conversation with other people, I prepare my next words to ensure I convey my message well.					
I ask clarifying questions if I am confused about what my conversation partners mean.					
I take into account cultural differences when talking with someone.					
I'm shocked to learn that what I'm trying to say has not been understood by everyone.					
In order to minimize misunderstandings, I make an effort to explain the core ideas that surround the topic I talk about.					
Before speaking, I consider what other people feel and how they might react.					
After writing an email or document, I like to check it for errors. When there are no mistakes, I then send it out.					
I attempt to understand other people's viewpoints when I have a conversation with them.					
I reach out to others through email for difficult problems because it is much easier and faster.					
I like to demonstrate my thoughts through charts.					
I choose the best method of communication before communicating with the other person.					

By evaluating these key components of your communication style, you can recognize your strengths and areas for improvement. Throughout the following chapters, we will discuss practical tips to address these areas.

It might look bleak for women in leadership, but considering how the evidence points to women being amazing leaders and communicators, the solution is relatively simple. Women need to actively work on their communication skills and help other women do the same. We are going to jump straight into this, in the next chapter, with body language.

2
Body Language and Nonverbal Cues

"Women are better at reading body language everywhere in the world. As a matter of fact, it is associated with the female hormone estrogen. Women are better at figuring out the tone of voice, reading your face, posture, and gesture."
– Helen Fisher

The fact that women are good at reading body language goes back to ancient times when men went out to hunt while women were more responsible for raising children. As babies don't know how to speak, women need to pay more attention to nonverbal cues in order to meet their baby's needs. We can still see this today when moms can differentiate between the tone and pitch of their baby's cries.

The Significance of Body Language

There are many statistics on body language and communication but one of the most frequently seen is the 55/38/7 formula proposed by Albert Mehrabian and his research into face-to-face conversations that broke down communication into 55% nonverbal, 38% vocal, and 7% words (Thompson, 2011).

Before we go deeper into learning about body language, we need to first understand what body language is. Body language—frequently enacted unconsciously instead of intentionally—is when a person uses facial expressions, eye contact, tone of voice, and gestures for nonverbal communication (Segal et al., 2023). Although understanding how to communicate effectively is essential for achieving success in life, your body language usually speaks louder than your words. Body language has been a significant form of communication since long before spoken language developed. It reveals our thoughts and feelings, even when we are silent. It is often a more accurate way to gauge a person's emotions and deeper feelings because elements of this form of communication are controlled by the subconscious.

It is important to give a good impression when we are communicating with other people. You may need to accomplish this by projecting positive and good body language. By displaying positive body language, you can demonstrate your eagerness to participate, comfort with facing obstacles, and self-confidence. This means that you will enable yourself to attract and take advantage of new opportunities when people are impressed with how you behave and speak. It is crucial to pay attention to how you carry yourself. Whether you are on a first date or in a business meeting, maintaining positive body language is a must. This will show that you are genuine, determined, and eager to learn new things.

Conversely, poor and negative body language may convey the wrong messages to other people. It could show that you are unwilling to participate, reluctant to face challenges, and unsure of your skills. It might also shut off the path to advancement and achievement. When you display negative body language, you risk losing other people's attention. Regardless of how interesting or crucial the points you try to make are, the right message won't be understood if it is presented in the wrong way.

The truth is that there are many benefits to gain when you understand how to read body language in the workplace. First, it encourages productivity. For example, as a female leader, you need to know the nonverbal cues that your team members display. When you look at their facial expressions, you might see that they lack motivation and are distracted. Then, you can make adjustments after determining what's holding them back from being productive. As a leader, you must know how to observe your team's emotions so that you can motivate them to do better.

Second, it fosters discipline. When you know how to communicate well with your team members, you can make sure that they perform their responsibilities well. When motivating them to work harder, you need to show them how serious their work is with the proper tone of voice and facial expressions. By doing this, you will convey the right message which makes your team realize how important it is to do their best.

Third, it saves your time and energy. A leader who knows how to use the proper body language to communicate effectively will save energy in explaining something to their team. With positive body language, your team will pay attention to what you have to say, so you won't need to waste time repeating yourself again.

Additionally, effectively reading and using body language minimizes misunderstanding. Without awareness of your communication style, your body language may contradict what you say. This is why, as a leader, you must learn to read the situation you are in and display the right body language to avoid misunderstanding around your team members.

Getting Better at Understanding Facial Expressions

There are seven facial expressions that are called micro-expressions. They occur for a fraction of a second and are extremely difficult to fake. The good thing about micro-expressions is that they are universal, so they will be expressed in similar ways across genders and cultures. What are these micro-expressions and how do you read them?

- **Sadness:**
    - It is not easy to fake sadness on your face, and in fact, it is the most difficult emotion to simulate. It can be identified when the lips pout and are down creating a frown, the jaw moves up, the cheeks are raised, and the eyebrows' inner corners are pulled in, then lifted.

- **Surprise:**
    - Imagine yourself being startled; the eyebrows need to be less tense and curved, the eyes are opened but the bottom eyelids are relaxed, the mouth wide open, and the teeth separate.

- **Anger:**
    - This micro-expression is expressed when the eyebrows are brought together and dropped, the lips are squeezed together, the eyes wide open, and the jaw moves forward.

- **Fear:**
  - This expression can be seen when the eyes are wide open, the eyebrows are brought together and elevated, and the lips are tightened.

- **Disgust:**
  - When you smell something unpleasant, your face will show disgust; the eyebrows are drawn together, the lips are pursed, and the nose or mouth is often covered with your hand.

- **Contempt:**
  - When you hold someone in contempt, you consider them to be below you (Saulsbery, 2023). This expression is shown when the mouth is raised only on one side of your face.

- **Happiness:**
  - This expression can happen when you receive good news or think of something nice. It is shown when someone is smiling; the cheeks are raised, the mouth can be closed or opened, the teeth can be visible, and the lips pursed together. Happiness can also be displayed through the Duchenne smile, which is perceived to be the most sincere sign of joy; this smile reaches the eyes and causes the crow's feet to form in the corners (Stanborough, 2019).

What Your Body Is Telling Others

In order to communicate with others, you need to know how you move your body. Your body needs to show the right message so that there is no misunderstanding during the communication process. Your eye contact and gestures when you talk are very important, and learning to effectively utilize these nuanced aspects of conversation can empower you to communicate clearly and confidently.

Eye Contact

Eye contact is a type of body language that occurs when people look directly into each other's eyes, and it is considered nonverbal communication, utilized to express a wide range of emotions (Eatough, 2021). It can be challenging to make eye contact sometimes, especially if you are neurodivergent. You may even feel uncomfortable, particularly if you do not have any strong connection with the audience or the other person. Have you attempted to make eye contact when speaking in front of an audience? Or how about when you are in a conversation with your colleague and you need to offer them your full attention? We all have done these before.

Why is it so essential to make eye contact when you try to communicate with others? Even when two individuals think they are listening closely to each other, it is still possible to have miscommunication. When eye contact is made during a conversation, generally, both parties can better concentrate on what is being said and read each other's expressions. This means the message can be understood better. When the speaker and listener understand each other, communication is also improved.

Making eye contact is also an approach to expressing respect. For instance, when someone is trying to tell you something important and you look into their eyes instead of looking at your phone, this will let them know that you care about what they have to say and that you are listening to the information being conveyed. When this happens, you establish trust and enhance your relationship.

Making eye contact in a conversation can also show that you are an honest and open person. Sometimes, you can see whether someone is lying or not by looking into their eyes. Eye contact can convey different emotions that cannot be expressed through words. When someone sees that you are an open person, trust can also be built.

But, you may be thinking, *how much eye contact is appropriate in a conversation?* You can utilize the 50–70 rule while speaking to somebody, which means that you need to maintain eye contact between 50% and 70% of the time throughout the entire discussion (Eatough, 2021). By doing this while someone is speaking, you also become good at active listening, which is another important aspect of effective communication.

When do we need to use eye contact? You do not have to make eye contact all the time. Eye contact can be made when you want to show the other person that you respect and understand what they are saying. When you make eye contact with the speaker, they will feel heard and seen which can boost their self-esteem. You can also do this when you want to emphasize a point in order to get the audience's attention back to you.

If you wish to learn how to make eye contact, the following are some tips that you can consider: Prior to saying anything in a discussion, first make eye contact with the other person. Once eye contact has been made, it will be easier to face them and communicate. Another tip is to hold eye contact for only four to five seconds to establish your confidence or make the other person comfortable (Rhymes, 2023). If you look at other people's eyes for too long, it can make them feel uncomfortable and they might also think that you are being invasive or aggressive. Additionally, if you want to break eye contact, you need to turn away slowly so that the other person does not feel bad or offended. The reality is that bettering your eye contact skills can be a long process. Starting with the people you are most comfortable with can help to ease the journey to enacting this skill in the workplace. You can practice with your friends or family members first.

Gestures

The first benefit of using gestures in communication is that it may help you avoid overthinking. When you move your body and use gestures when speaking, you can communicate information more effectively. Using gestures will also help you connect with your audience. Nobody enjoys it if someone is talking without moving their body at all. This makes the audience's thoughts stray away, and they will lose interest in what you have to say. Likewise, a speaker who is constantly fidgeting is simply distracting. Learning to effectively utilize gestures involves finding a happy medium of movement.

During a conversation, people will observe your gestures. They will remember more of what you say when you use proper gestures. When someone talks and you use gestures, they will feel like you respect and understand the message they try to communicate. Therefore, gestures, as a whole, help you become more active in a conversation, and this will make you a better communicator.

Some gestures are easy to understand, and some are not. Culture plays a huge role in interpreting gestures, and in the workplace, there is diversity that will need to be navigated. Moreover, gestures should be used with care. There are several things to pay attention to when learning about gestures, including your arms and legs, postures, and personal spaces:
- **Arms and legs:**
    - The placement of one's arms and legs are important in communication. When someone's arms are crossed, the person might be defensive about something. When the legs are crossed, they may be at-

tempting to stay away from an individual that the person might dislike or feel uncomfortable around. One indication that someone is feeling good and is prepared to take in information is if their arms are by their sides and in an open position. Additionally, someone who has their feet set firmly on the ground shows that they are ready to listen to the conversation.

- **Personal space:**
  - Have you ever felt uneasy because somebody approached you just a little bit too closely? This happens when you feel like your personal space is being invaded. Everyone has different boundaries when it comes to their personal space, so it's important to pay attention to a person's behavior when you stand next to them. If they look uncomfortable, you need to move away a little bit.

- **Posture:**
  - Someone can be seen to be actively participating, attentive, and open during the conversation when they raise their shoulders and sit up straight. However, if you see that someone is slouching and not sitting straight, they may feel anxious, tense, or upset during the discussion. To understand someone's posture, you need to know how to observe their position when talking to them. Likewise, it is important to be aware of what you are unintentionally communicating with your posture.

Other Vocal, Nonverbal, and Habitual Cues That Impact Communication

Paralanguage is the way we produce sounds and the variations in our voices. Research was conducted in which 4,000 people listened to nine speakers and were asked to identify their characteristics based on the voices; the results showed that the listeners were able to identify the sex, age, and job of these presenters accurately, which was very surprising (Edwards, 2023). Humans use paralanguage in their daily lives; the various types of paralanguage convey a message to the listeners, and they also affect people's emotions in the process (Arora, 2017):

- **Upspeak:**

    - This is the term for an increasing pitch of the voice, typically near the end of a statement. Women are the ones who typically use this paralanguage. But this needs to be stopped because when overused, upspeak can imply a lack of assertiveness.

- **Intonation:**

    - The rise and fall of voice pitch is referred to as intonation, and it is crucial for asking questions (Nordquist, 2019). Everybody has their own intonation, and there is no way a person can speak without using any intonation at all.

- **Lowered voice:**

    - In dating, women usually like when men have a deep voice. This type of man typically shows dominance and authority over other men who do not have low voices (Edwards, 2023). Women, however, must be careful with this tactic as a deepening of our pitch can often inadvertently come across as seductive.

- **Silence:**
  - Have you ever given your partner the silent treatment after a fight? It is very common for people to use silence when they are upset. However, as this cuts off communication—and thus, the ability to resolve problems—it is a form of passive aggression when used in this way. Instead, it is best to use silence in brief doses as an opportunity to allow your audience to digest information.

- **Humor:**
  - This happens when you make a joke and other people laugh. When you can laugh together, you can connect with each other better.

- **Scoffing:**
  - This happens when someone is making fun of another person. They might think what someone else says is stupid or ridiculous, so they breathe out dismissively to make a mockery of it.

- **Stuttering:**
  - Those who stutter might be anxious talking in public or have a neurological difficulty disrupting their speech patterns. Sadly, this is highly stigmatized, and often, a person with a stutter may even refuse to have social interactions with others because they feel ashamed of their stuttering. Remember to have patience with a person with a stutter—be that yourself or an interlocutor.

- **Accent and dialect:**
  - Every country, region, or culture speaks differently, and they each have their own accent and dialect.

However, accent bias can happen because of this. People usually have prejudices toward certain accents. Those from a minority group might get discriminated against because of their accent.

- **Mumbling:**

    o Mumbling can happen when someone is shy or unsure of themselves or others in a social situation.

- **Vocal cadence:**

    o This refers to the voice's flow. For instance, pausing when speaking creates a rhythm. When someone does this, they might be stopping to think of their next words or simply allowing a moment for the audience to catch up.

- **Fast-talking:**

    o Have you ever suddenly talked fast in a social setting? This might happen because you feel nervous. If you do this often, you can try to relax and calm yourself down before continuing to talk again.

- **Tongue clicking:**

    o This occurs when someone wants to show annoyance or frustration. For instance, if your friend is doing something silly, you might show your disapproval through tongue-clicking. However, be aware that some cultures have tongue clicks, also referred to as click consonants, incorporated into their language.

- **Vocal pitch:**

    o People may raise or low their pitch when talking. Typically, lower-pitch voices are considered to be soothing, and higher pitch may sound angry or nervous (Edwards, 2023).

- **Incessant talking:**
  - This type of paralanguage happens when someone keeps talking nonstop. There are some reasons why they do this; they might feel so excited about something that they cannot stop, or they are so arrogant that they do not want to give anyone else a chance to talk.

- **Sneering:**
  - Someone may sneer when they feel angry or irritated, and they expose their teeth with this expression.

Reading the Whole Room

Before putting all of this into practice, it is crucial that you consider a few things. The first is that you need to understand a person's baseline for communication. A baseline is someone's normal body language when they are relaxed. Getting a baseline will allow you to look for anomalies. Some people naturally speak faster, while others may blink more frequently; because these are a part of that person's baseline, they should not be taken as signs of anxiety or excitement when noticed during conversation. On the other hand, if you notice a person who normally speaks quite quickly is slowing down their rate of speech, this may be a sign that they are making an important point and want to be sure of being understood. All of us share many basic characteristics, but not everyone perceives, moves, behaves, speaks, expresses, reacts, or interacts with others in exactly the same ways (Swami, 2022). This is why you need to observe and understand a person's baseline before trying to build a good rapport with them through communication.

As a leader, you need to know each of your team member's baseline. Once you understand this, you will be able to realize when a change is happening. When you are attentive enough, you will see when someone is under stress or anxiety because their body language strays outside of their baseline. For example, when a team member who is usually outgoing and talkative suddenly becomes quiet and reserved, you will think that there is something wrong. This skill helps you plan the necessary interventions to help your team members.

It is also important to look for clusters of behavior rather than focus on one movement or gesture. Likewise, it is helpful to be mindful of the context in which body language occurs. It would be wrong to assume that a person is feeling defensive when they have only crossed their arms because the office is cold. A cluster would be a group of actions that indicate how a person is feeling. If you keep in mind that someone's general demeanor is significantly more insightful than any particular gesture, you will improve your ability to understand body language (Goman, 2023).

When you can understand how to look for clusters, you can read a situation easily. For example, when you ask a team member if they are okay after you take them off a project and they say they are fine, by observing their clusters of behaviors, you can realize that their body language says otherwise. Instead of taking your team members' words at face value, you can then decide to promise to assign them to a different project or further explain your reasoning for reassigning them to help ease any tension or disappointment.

Finally, body language has to be put into context. It is all very well and good to be capable of recognizing the signs of discomfort, but we cannot assume that the source of discomfort is us. You need to be aware of the conversation, the environment, and possible past experiences. Multiple factors can alter a situational analysis before you can identify a reliable solution.

If you are the leader of a team and see that one of your members is showing discomfort, you have to take a moment to assess the context. After understanding the context, you can try to remove the source of the discomfort and see if they feel at ease. For instance, when you bring up a sensitive topic and a team member becomes tense and uneasy, you can stop talking about it for a period of time and observe if they are more relaxed. As a leader, you have a responsibility to take care of your team members, and when you know how to read their body language, you can create a better working environment for them and they will respect you more.

After reading this chapter, are you interested in reading your colleagues' body language? That's great! However, you should not rush into the application of this knowledge because this is a skill that takes time and practice. This is now the time for you to pay attention to your own nonverbal cues. At first, you do not have to get another person involved because you can start practicing in the mirror. After understanding your own nonverbal cues, you can move on to people in your inner circle, such as your friends or family members. Perhaps, you have a coworker who is close to you that you can practice this skill with. This doesn't mean that you should entirely avoid applying this skill to the people in the office right away; the thing to remember is that you need time and practice before you can read body language signs accurately. You might not even feel comfortable applying a skill that you have not mastered yet. Once you feel more at ease and feel confident in fluently reading body language, you may then begin using this skill in your workplace.

With all of this in mind, we will now move on to communication styles and take a closer look at the actual language we use.

3
Taking Your Voice to the Next Level

"I found I was more confident when I stopped trying to be someone else's definition of beautiful and started being my own." – Remington Miller

Nowadays, women are always bombarded with so many tips on how to be a boss. This is not always bad, but it causes us to lose sight of our true selves and try to imitate other people. If you wish to be more confident in your personal and professional life, you need to stay true to yourself. Stop trying to follow someone else's definition of success. When you know who you are deep down, this confidence will spill into your voice.

What Is Your Communication Style?

Every one of us has a different way of communicating, and there are five primary communication styles that are most common. Our style will depend on whether we like to communicate in a direct or indirect way. Because people have various communication styles, disputes and miscommunication might arise easily. When you can determine your own style and those of the people you interact with, it will be easier for you to communicate effectively.

Assertive

The assertive communication style is regarded to be the best style in a professional setting. Someone who has this style has strong opinions and communicates them with conviction, but they ensure that they do not demean or dominate the discussion (Martins, 2022). They are good at being direct without hurting other people's feelings. They show confidence while expressing wants and needs. Instead of using coercion or pushing boundaries, they like to reach mutual understanding by listening to the other person and saying what they want in detail.

People who have an assertive style typically have good self-esteem and self-confidence, and they avoid using passive or hostile language when speaking. They do not let their feelings get in the way of the discussion because they know emotions can negatively influence their judgment; yet, they still allow space for emotional reactions to be discussed appropriately. They also have a positive outlook and are composed when trying to find solutions to the issues at hand. Rather than only focusing on what they want, they will choose to hear different perspectives and make decisions after considering all of them carefully. They are also more trusted by the people around them because they respect everyone.

Tips to Become More Assertive

Everyone can become an assertive communicator, regardless of where they start. As explained before, high self-esteem and self-confidence are the foundation of an assertive communication style. This means that it is important for you to recognize your value and appreciate your wishes and rights.

In addition, assertiveness goes hand in hand with respecting others and their opinions in discussions. This involves encouraging others in the decision-making process and asking them for help in dealing with issues rather than doing everything by yourself. If you ever feel frustrated or irritated when someone makes a mistake, avoid shouting, screaming, or becoming hostile toward them. When this happens, it is important to process your own emotional response and relax before speaking so that your words do not undermine your attempt to be assertive.

Instead of pointing fingers at others by saying, "Your work was awful," an assertive person phrases their feedback using "I" statements and addresses solutions rather than problems such as by saying, "I have faith in your skills. This could be better [identify the areas of improvement], so what can I do to assist you with your project?" By doing this, the other person will feel respected, acknowledge their mistakes, and better themselves in the future, knowing that you are there to help them grow. If you are accusatory, either you will crumble their confidence and they will be scared of working with you again, or they will become defensive and meet your justified criticism with anger.

Assertive communicators also know how and when to say no. If someone wants you to take over a task and your workload is already too much, you must learn to say no instead of agreeing because you feel bad. You need to establish and enforce your boundaries, and if they ever cross them, there needs to be consequences.

Passive

This communication style is also named the "submissive" style, and people who favor this style are often called people-pleasers (Nwanne, 2023). Those who have this style are usually quiet and laid-back. They also like to remove themselves from conflicts because they are highly uncomfortable with facing them. However, having a passive style is not always great. These people typically don't know how to express their thoughts or ideas for fear of being criticized, which may lead to frustration and burnout. Since they dislike disagreements and will do anything to steer clear of them, they usually let others have their way leading everything. When they are intimidated, they will not resort to violence or anger, but just brush it off with humor.

In a professional setting, the passive style can be utilized in response to hostile communication in the workplace. When a coworker or client is being aggressive to you, you can use this to calm the situation down if the other styles do not work. Moreover, if you have to deal with passive people, you can help motivate them to express what they are actually thinking by being welcoming, pleasant, and kind. These people also like to avoid talking in groups, so you will need to encourage them, many times privately, to share their ideas or they may never express themselves.

Tips to be Less Passive

You might think that when you become more passive, you are kinder and will show people more respect. However, this will make your communication skills suffer. If you want to be better at communicating, you must accept that you have value and can also participate in discussions. You are a human with thoughts and not a statue with no opinions, so you need to be able to voice your ideas.

When you disagree with someone else's opinions, you should not be afraid of voicing your disagreement. I know that it may be difficult to face conflicts when you feel safer avoiding them, but things will never get better if you do not contribute. The other person might also respond positively, and this can benefit both of you. However, you need to listen closely to them before expressing your opinions and avoid talking over them. If you are worried that expressing your perspective could be perceived as condescending or arrogant, you can lighten the situation with a smile. The discussion can also flow better when you speak up, and you will not build any resentment toward anyone because conflict can be resolved through discussion rather than simply continuing to build tension.

Aggressive

Just like the name implies, those who have this style can be aggressive, hostile, and motivated by the desire to gain the upper hand no matter what. They often think that their opinions are the only right ones. They consider themselves to be more important than others. It does not mean that their opinions are not good, but because they deliver them in an aggressive way, others might not be able to see their value.

People who come in contact with people like this may feel frightened, intimidated, and overpowered. Others may respond negatively to an aggressive communicator, regardless of the message being communicated, simply because it was delivered in a terrible manner. Perhaps, you have seen many leaders use this style and instead of looking brave or strong, they become overbearing and scary to their employees. When someone tries to disagree with them, they will not accept it and become disrespectful. No one can trust a leader with this communication style because they do not value others. They like to use loud voices when talking and do not pay attention to others' boundaries. Unlike people who favor the assertive style, aggressive communicators don't care about another person's feelings as long as they can get what they want in the discussion.

Tips to be Less Aggressive

For a discussion to work, it must be a two-way exchange. You need to identify your communication style, and if you recognize that you have a tendency to use an aggressive style, it is important to work on changing it. The best place to begin is by considering what drives you to be aggressive in communication. You may then try to be more welcoming to others, kinder, and less intimidating. It is also vital to actively listen to others and genuinely appreciate their thoughts and concerns.

Moreover, practicing showing empathy for other people is a key aspect of reducing aggression in your communication. You can think about how others will react to your behavior and words. If you can be aware of how harsh your words can be, you will understand how they feel. Watch out for your body language as well; if your gestures show aggressiveness and your voice is too loud, you need to step back and try to relax. When you are calmer, others will respond to you more positively. Additionally, you have to shift your perspective: In a discussion, the aim is to address the issue, not to win a debate. You have to collaborate with others so that you can be more successful in communicating.

Passive-Aggressive

As its name implies, this communication style includes elements of passive and aggressive ways. Someone who has this style will attempt to appear passive and laid-back, but they are aggressive on the inside, which bubbles through in their actions. Although they may look kind and friendly on the outside, they are really acting out of bitterness and frustration. They also like to use sarcasm and enjoy spreading rumors. Passive-aggressive people will not openly express their disagreement or dislike for anything; instead, they will hide their feelings and talk behind people's backs.

Although they express their anger and irritation in these subtle ways, they will still negatively impact their image around others which makes people unwilling to collaborate with them. These people are usually very toxic in professional settings, and others do not trust them or are scared to offend them in any way. This communication style is not good for a workplace because it can disrupt the flow in which people work.

Tips to be Less Passive-Aggressive

This style is frequently used to avoid conflict, although it is actually an aggressive behavior. If you find yourself having this style of communication, it will be important for you to practice properly expressing your thoughts and being more direct. You need to keep in mind that not every disagreement leads to conflict. Being more honest about your concerns will often allow you to find a quick solution with the other person and avoid the perceived need for passive-aggressive interactions.

You must try to determine the source of your anger. Do you think others are not paying attention to you? Do you think your ideas are being ignored too often? Let others know about these concerns. In a discussion, are you reacting angrily, or are you genuinely trying to fix the issue? Change the way you handle conflict, and attempt to put more of an emphasis on optimistic, problem-solving ideas.

For instance, if you keep making mistakes on a project, your coworker might ask you about it. Instead of being passive-aggressive and bombarding your coworker with guilt-inducing excuses, you need to ask them to elaborate on which parts you get wrong. After they explain, if you do not agree, you need to describe your perspectives on the matter. When this discussion ends, you both will find out where the issue truly lies and try to resolve it together. We all have been passive-aggressive and petty at times, but if we want to be successful, we need to express our thoughts respectfully in our workplace.

Manipulative

Someone who has this communication style manipulates the discussion's conclusion and, in turn, the behavior of those around them by using deception, persuasion, and trickery (Nwanne, 2023). Manipulative people hardly express what they intend to say. They like to conceal their true intentions beneath multiple guises to gain their desired outcomes. It is possible that others are unaware of this deception.

This type of behavior is sometimes described as being dishonest, and in many cases, this is an extreme form of passive-aggression in which the communicator resorts to deception to avoid open conflict while still imposing their own views. When someone finds out that they have been duped by a manipulative person, they will never trust this person again.

Manipulative people are aware of what they need and want and how to acquire them. However, instead of communicating to others openly and with transparency, they choose to deceive others in order to accomplish their objectives. They know that they can get more by tricking people.

A manipulative person needs to be guided toward becoming assertive. They know how to accomplish what they want, and if they care more about other people's feelings and respect others, they will receive better outcomes. It is a win-win situation for them because they reach their goals and establish better relationships with others.

Tips to be Less Manipulative

In the short term, being manipulative may help gain you everything you wish short term, but you will only gain the hatred and mistrust of your coworkers later on. You need to be careful if you are manipulative because it might backfire on you. You must become conscious of how you affect others and analyze your motivations if you want to improve your communication skills. Rather than relying on psychological manipulation to persuade somebody to provide their assistance, you must ask them in person if they are willing to do it. Additionally, you need to look at how you interact with your coworkers to see if you are manipulating them in subtle ways.

It is vital for you to work on expressing yourself more clearly to others. Likewise, it is important to learn to tolerate a certain amount of disappointment; we cannot always get what we want, and manipulating others into constantly meeting our requests is *not* okay. During your transformation, some people might not believe you at first; many people are likely to believe that your new "honesty kick" is yet another form of manipulation. However, you can convince them that you are being sincere by being consistent and attempting not to go back to your old ways so that people can trust you more.

There Is No Such Thing as "Winging It"

Have you heard of the 6P rule? Prior proper planning prevents poor performance. Having a plan helps us to communicate ideas in a confident way. Let's learn how to plan for a meeting, especially if you are a leader.

Planning for a Leadership Meeting

The leader who is in charge of making presentations and organizing a meeting may find these tasks to be very stressful at times. There are many things that you need to prepare, such as how you can speak confidently, clearly, and successfully during an important meeting. It can be a difficult task to convince others that your team is working well and moving in the right direction. The following are some things that you need to prepare before attending a leadership meeting.

The first thing to do is to understand the goals of the audience. For instance, if you need to attend a managerial meeting with other managers and your bosses, you have to know what the agenda is and prepare accordingly. Understanding your audience allows you to effectively address their concerns and avoid wasting time in the process.

After that, you need to clearly identify your presentation's overall goal. The agenda of the meeting will largely guide you in this. After knowing the goal, you have to consider the most effective ways to accomplish it. Once you have prepared for the presentation, you can practice it in front of the mirror to make sure that you are confident enough in your communication style in the meeting.

Within the meeting, it is crucial to display competence in front of the participants. A leader needs to show their capabilities because their success is determined by notable achievements. You can display your competence by being diligent and well-prepared. By understanding the goal of the meeting, the company, and your position, you will project competence to others.

Furthermore, you can improve your display of competence by brainstorming potential questions that might be asked prior to the meeting. You can consider various questions about individuals, company culture, business goals, and processes relating to the topic and goal of your presentation. If any of those questions come up during the meeting, it will be easier for you to answer them without pause.

Lastly, you need to be open to criticism and feedback. This step is very important because there will always be criticism of whatever you do. When someone provides you with feedback, you should not feel offended. You have to be honest and open. If a leader is not ready to accept criticism, they will never advance. You need to be ready for feedback and express gratitude for it.

Preparing for a Presentation

A crucial aspect of a successful presentation is preparation. Days or weeks before the meeting, you need to devote time and energy to preparation and planning. In addition to helping you feel more confident, thorough preparation will help you reach your goals and convey the message intended.

After you have planned out your presentation, You will have to rehearse it. However, you need to avoid memorizing the whole script. If you memorize a presentation, you might forget it when you feel nervous or anxious. What you need to do is to understand the key points so that your presentation can flow more naturally. Try to practice in front of your friends or family, and ask for feedback on what you need to improve.

Preparing an opening line is also essential. An opening line is what can capture the audience's attention. Memorizing this line will help you boost your confidence. Many people typically feel better and more confident after they say their opening line which removes their worries as well.

It can also be helpful to have a backup plan. Sometimes, things might not go as smoothly as we have planned. Nothing is worse than discovering your laptop does not work or the projector does not connect to it. To avoid these instances, you need to have a backup to feel more secure because when you have prepared for everything, you can let go of "what if" anxieties.

When you have a presentation to make, you need to arrive at the meeting earlier than others. This will allow you to ensure that everything is ready or make changes if you find any errors. By doing this, you can also feel less pressured or anxious because you have some time to relax and prepare your mental state before the presentation.

The next tip is to organize your presentation according to the time allotted. Sometimes, we might speak faster than normal when we feel nervous, which will make us finish much earlier with some of our listeners feeling rushed and confused. We need to prepare sufficient materials in case this happens.

Other times, we may feel the need to add more information than planned for, creating a longer meeting than agreed upon with information overload for our audience. This is why rehearsing the presentation is important so that you can see its duration from the beginning to the end and make changes where needed.

Using Your Words Wisely

In a professional setting, you need to pay attention to the words you use and utilize them wisely. Your career advancement can depend on your word choices, so it is important to know what to use and what to avoid. Let's explore them so that you can sound more professional.

The Use of Pronouns, Adjectives, and Sensory Words

The types of pronouns you use in a conversation matter. Your choice of pronouns will reveal different meanings for your audience. Let's take a look at an example: You have a friend who has a new employee at their company. When you ask them, "How is the new guy?" they may respond in different ways:

- They might say, "I love working with the new guy."

    o This means that your friend concentrates on their own experience and puts themselves first by utilizing the pronoun "I."

- They may express, "He is good at his job, and he is friendly to others."

    o The focus on "he" and "his job" in this sentence indicates that your friend cares about the new guy, his professional performance, and how he behaves around others.

- **They might say, "The outfit the new guy wore was nice and clean."**
  - This use of a stand-in title and no pronouns means that your friend focuses on an object related to the new employee, rather than the employee himself. This imposition of linguistic distance indicates that either there is a problem with the new guy and your friend is scrambling for something positive to say, or they were really impressed by how he dresses.

The next aspect of language that is important to consider is adjectives. In fact, we can utilize adjectives either with or against a person. This is why we need to listen to the other person's preferred uplifting words. For example, a client may often use words like "amazing," "wonderful," "excellent," or "outstanding" when speaking. You can use these adjectives to your advantage by mirroring them when closing a deal, promoting a new product, or attempting to motivate that client.

Sensory words—used to describe what we experience—are an equally important aspect of our language usage. These can include how you see, feel, smell, taste, and hear things around you. People have their own choice of sensory words, and they might prefer one over another. For example, if someone is an auditory person, they will say, "That sounds nice." If someone is physically motivated, they may say, "That feels amazing." By observing the sensory word choices of your colleagues and clients, you can make language choices of your own that appeal to and motivate the people around you.

Filler Words

Filler words are sounds like "ohh," "umm," and "ah" or words such as "you know" and "like." There are different reasons why we use fillers: They might be a sign that we are thinking, or they can be used to show we are listening, hesitating, or feeling disappointed. However, many people associate filler words with uncertainty and a lack of confidence. Therefore, these words shouldn't be used in public speaking, which is why it is essential to plan any presentation well.

Many of us use filler words out of habit. We can easily hear these words in the media or the people around us. Because we are often exposed to them in our daily lives, we pick them up unintentionally. When something turns into a habit, we will use or do it spontaneously without thinking.

Filler words like "ah" and "umm" do sometimes serve an important purpose as they can be used to indicate that you are thinking. For instance, when you use "umm" in casual conversation, it can signal to others that you are assembling your thoughts and that they need to refrain from speaking until you have finished.

Filler words can also be used to make a discussion less tense. When you are telling someone about sensitive things or something unpleasant, filler words may be used as a linguistic "cushion." For instance, if your colleague failed to get promoted to a managerial position and you might soften the news by saying, "I was told to let you know that, umm, you were not selected to be the manager."

Not all filler words are terrible, so please don't be scared of using them occasionally because they can add valuable meanings. However, it is important to be aware of when the use of filler words is detrimental—for example, if they are overused. You can use these words and phrases as much as you please in informal situations, but it is not recommended to say them too often in professional settings.

When presenting something in your workplace, it is normal to sometimes say "umm" or "ah." However, if you are too casual and occupy every pause with filler words, you risk losing the audience's interest because you might look nervous and anxious. It is hard for an audience to trust you if your language indicates that you don't trust yourself, so you need to be aware of these filler words and use them appropriately.

What Message Does Your Appearance Convey?

You might think that to look professional, you need to wear a pencil skirt suit and a pair of heels. But not all of us have the coordination to wear 6-inch heels all day long. Heels are an absolute killer and affect my mood and, worse, my posture. It is hard to feel confident when you are not comfortable wearing your outfit, and we are all capable of looking our best without needing to suffer for it. To go against an old adage: Beauty is *not* pain.

As a successful leader, you do not want the topic of conversation to be your appearance; people should be focused on your messages. This is why you need to pay attention to what you wear and how to dress for the occasion. Even though you are not a celebrity who has to dress to impress, female leaders still have to be in the spotlight. As professional women in leadership positions, we need to dress appropriately so that our message can be taken seriously. The following are some tips that can help you to effectively portray leadership through your clothing choices:

- **Being fashionable within your company's dress code:**

- Some companies have strict dress rules, while others are more lenient. Whichever way this may lean, you must be properly put together in front of people. When choosing your clothes, it is helpful to choose good quality, timeless materials, such as linen, cotton, and silk, and tailoring if needed so that the clothes fit your unique shape both comfortably and appealingly. It's worthwhile investing a little in your clothing and exploring what styles make you feel at your best.

- **Choosing the right colors:**
  - When choosing colors, the first thing to consider is what makes us feel comfortable. However, we should also be mindful of what color we wear to important events so that we can attract the appropriate type and amount of attention. One such example is ensuring that our color palette mirrors our professional stance: For instance, we would want to wear something blue while representing Lowe's Home Improvement and orange if representing Home Depot, but not vice versa. Exploring color theory and visual palettes is a fun way to discover what story you'd like to display through your professional fashion.

- **Being flexible for the occasion:**
  - We don't always have to dress formally at work—for example, if you have a casual event at work where people dress in only jeans and shirts. Likewise, your company may host gala-style events at which black tie attire might be necessary. It is important to always gauge the level of formality and dress accordingly.

- **Making yourself comfortable:**

- Most importantly, your clothing choices rely on what looks good on you and conveys the right image that you are comfortable in. We should not force ourselves to wear something uncomfortable or makes us feel fake to ourselves.

Let's take a look at an example: Vanessa had just been promoted to a managerial position at her office. Before getting the role, she did not really care about what she wore and never tried to impress anyone. However, once she had a new position, she strived to impress people and "prove herself" with how she looked. Every day, she would dress very professionally in suits, skirts, and heels. She knew that these things were uncomfortable for her, but she was willing to impress others no matter what. One day, the office held a casual outing, and everyone else chose to dress...well...comfortably casual. But Vanessa did not want that, fearing that any deviation from her high-class norm would cause people to again see her as what she perceived as the regular unnoticeable employee she'd once been. She stuck with her professional yet uncomfortable clothes. That day, people looked at her strangely, and this made her feel insecure. All the confidence she had built went down the drain. One of her coworkers then pulled her aside and kindly communicated to her that she looked great, but that her outfit made it seem like she was bringing work to an outside-of-work occasion. Vanessa realized that she was trying too hard to continuously fit a narrative that she was projecting from within herself into her workplace, and it had backfired on her. After that event, she thought hard about what made her who she is, and decided to balance comfort with a new polished look that worked for her interests instead of what she perceived was expected of her. Thankfully, just dressing more casually cute at times made her feel both comfortable and professional, and in turn helped her to be seen as more confident and approachable from her coworkers. Now that's a fashion statement!

In today's modern world, communication is not limited to interactions with other people in the office. Whether you are working for a multinational company or running a team using project management software, digital interactions count. In the following chapter, we will look at how to make your digital communication heard and understood!

4
Communication in the Digital World

"Technology is a useful servant but a dangerous master." –
Christian Lous Lange

Because of the prevalence of technology in the modern workplace, we have to learn how to use it and get the most out of its communication benefits. However, it's important not to become so reliant on the screens that we forget or become uncomfortable communicating face-to-face.

Pros and Cons of the Digital Workplace

According to a recent study, 66% of employees wasted 30 minutes to an hour each day trying to keep up with conversations, 75% felt the constant notifications were a distraction, and 42% said they missed out on important information because of ineffective communication tools (Tran, 2018). It is true that social networking has its benefits nowadays, but there are also some disadvantages to depending on it. Let's explore the pros and cons of the digital workplace.

Pros

These days, technology is used so frequently in both our personal and professional lives; companies are swiftly adapting to compete with startup businesses that have implemented a digital workplace from the beginning. Now, people don't have to meet in person to communicate; they have a digital space where they can contact each other.

The first advantage of this change is that it improves communication. Connecting becomes easier in a digital workplace because you can communicate at any time and in any place. There are so many apps that can be used to connect and message people in a professional setting, such as *Slack* and *Microsoft Teams*. Those who work remotely can also get updated information about the company even though they are not in the office. Through these apps, companies can share modifications, announcements, or general knowledge with their employees easily. This promotes clarity and transparency because everybody receives their information at the same time.

A digital workplace also helps companies to find and keep talent. Most companies struggle constantly with employee retention and turnover, particularly those without a solid reputation. Many also still have trouble motivating their current employees, overseeing their overall performance, and developing a work environment that draws top talent to apply. Companies now have the chance to use a digital workplace to organize workflows and information and develop a social network as well as a communication system, which will build their reputation and draw top talent to their side.

Furthermore, it will increase the company's revenue. With a digital workplace, it will be easier for companies to save resources and time in business operations. Oftentimes, employees have a hard time obtaining information in a traditional setting. Through modern communication platforms, they can find information easily without having to waste time and energy moving around the office making face-to-face queries to individuals. With the internet, employees can also find new information through fast-speed search engines.

Cons

After learning about the advantages of a digital workplace, we can now move on to its disadvantages. As previously explained, enhancing digital communication and productivity throughout the company is the primary objective of implementing a digital workplace. However, this means that employees don't communicate with each other in person anymore. Since we have *Zoom* and *Google Meet* for video calls these days, people do not have to meet in real life to have meetings. This also indicates that people have fewer social interactions because they only rely on the digital workplace for communication. As a result, employees may feel more lonely and be unmotivated when they need to meet people in person.

A digital workplace also makes people dependent on it. There is no guarantee that the internet we rely on will function without error. We use technology daily and carry out our responsibilities with its help all the time. Most companies also make technology the heart of their operations. This dependency can lead to disaster if something goes wrong. Until the problem is fixed, the company will not be able to function at all.

Technology is always evolving, which means that companies will also need to train their employees to use new technologies. The morale of the employees may suffer, in turn, because they need to keep up with the continuous change and are expected to adjust to new developments. The truth is that this might make employees unmotivated to work on their tasks when they have to keep learning new things.

A Guide to Choosing Communication and Project Management Software

As a leader, it is important for you to know how to manage communication and projects for your team. Effectively managing team collaboration is the most essential part of success. Before exploring the ways to choose the right communication and project management software, it is helpful to understand the benefits that can be gained from this kind of software:

- Better project planning:

    o Planning a new project can take time. By using project management software, you can make projects simpler no matter how big or small they are. You can simply plan and arrange the projects on schedule and collect them in one location for the team to find.

- Improved resource management:

    o A crucial part of project management is its budget. By utilizing project management software, you can check and handle the budget easily from the beginning of the project to its completion. You can better monitor the expenses and pinpoint areas that need to be fixed.

- Optimized task management:

    o When a leader doesn't know how to manage projects, their team members will suffer. With project management software, you can delegate tasks more easily. There will be no confusion among your team members because you can arrange what they need to do from the start. To ensure that jobs are finished on time, you may also establish deadlines, to-do lists, and time trackers for every team member.

Now that you know the benefits of project management software, it is time to learn how to choose the right one for your team. Let's explore some crucial elements to look for:
- **Helps with tracking projects and managing tasks:**
    - Projects need to be turned into tasks. Therefore, having a system that makes it simple and effective to manage them all in one place will assist us complete the projects on schedule. We may assign tasks and keep track of them with ease using project management software that is equipped with a task management tool.
- **Provides simple communication:**
    - Your team needs to be informed directly if there are any modifications to the projects or tasks. By keeping everyone in the loop, your team can find solutions as soon as an issue arises. A dependable and effective project management tool should send notifications to all members through their devices so that no one misses out on information.
- **Easy to use:**
    - The software needs to be easy to learn. New users need to be able to use it right away without much training. Most companies probably do not have the time or resources to teach a new project management tool. Because of this, we must select a system that will be simple to set up and integrate into our workplace.

- **Offers a task-report tool:**
  - You should choose a tool that will encourage every member to report their tasks' progress. This will allow you to evaluate the team every step of the way. You may view every element of the project and make plans for how you will proceed moving forward. When you can track the team and their tasks, you may also see their performance.

- **Supports collaboration:**
  - The software needs to foster collaboration among the team members. This means that no matter how big the projects are, the team should be able to work together even remotely. This will allow the team to remain informed about all project advancements and to offer suggestions at any point in the project's progress.

- **Includes a feature for time tracking:**
  - To complete a project on time, you need to find software that can track everyone's time. You can see the duration your team spends on each task by using time tracking as well. Then, you may make better use of your time and devote more to tasks that demand it.

- **Easy to customize:**
  - It is usually helpful to have certain features that can be modified. The tool needs to be adaptable to the company's needs. Therefore, you must pay attention to the degree of customization that the tool provides.

- **Has an integration feature:**

- The software needs to be able to connect to other apps. This means that you do not have to move around to look at other apps on your computer, such as *Google Drive* or *Outlook*.

- **Priced within your budget:**
    - This is the most important thing to pay attention to because the cost consideration is quite vital if you are running a small company that does not have a big budget. Some tools might be too pricey, so you need to do your research.

How to Improve Your Written Communication

Written communication is hard because of the lack of nonverbal cues. This means that it is a lot easier for messages to be misunderstood—more specifically, the tone of a message. The readers can quickly make assumptions and respond in a way that hinders effective communication. Because we are often busy and rushing through our written communication, time is not taken to check for mistakes or evaluate if the wording is appropriate. The following are some tips to consider if you want to improve your written communication.

Seeking Help

You should not be scared to seek assistance if you think your writing needs work. Like any skill you want to get better at, your writing skills also need time and energy to improve. You can go to your supervisor or coworker to seek help. They will be pleased that you have come to them for help because it means that you trust them. Before sending an important document, you might ask someone to proofread or edit it so that there are no mistakes.

Keeping Notes of Thoughts and Ideas

When working, it is helpful to have a notebook with you at all times. This will allow you to write down any new ideas that come up. Then, when you need to compile your thoughts in an email or report, you can review the notebook again to get more facts. The message you are trying to communicate will be more impactful if it is backed up by relevant resources and notes. Your writing abilities will improve when you can offer accurate information in an email or document.

Editing and Proofreading

When it comes to writing, there is no such thing as too much editing. Before writing, try to create a list of what aspects you need to edit and arrange them. After writing, you'll need to check for grammar and spelling mistakes, the tone of the writing, the choice of words, etc. This will ensure that the message you want to convey can be easily understood by the readers. Once you find that the message is clear, review the text once more and make any necessary changes. General wisdom dictates that it is best to edit and proofread your own work around four times to avoid any mistakes. This is because we often initially read what we *meant to* write, rather than what is actually on the page. You may also find that reading your work aloud will help you to be more aware of any errors as you will literally *hear* the mistakes.

Reading

To be better at writing, you need to spend more time reading. So, well done: By reading this book, you are already helping yourself! When you read, you will encounter knowledge and vocabulary that you have not learned before. This will, in turn, improve your writing as you find new words or facts to add to your next message. In a professional setting, you can keep notes in meetings or read business articles so that you can become more skilled in your field, which will also affect your writing skill as you practice.

Seeing Things from the Reader's Perspectives

When writing, we must take the reader's viewpoint into account. You should consider the background knowledge they are likely to have on the subject because a client, for instance, will probably need a jargon-free explanation whereas a colleague will be familiar with industry terms. Understanding the type of readers that will read your written communication will enable you to know what words to choose and what tone to apply. You may also ask another person to read your writing and make changes according to their feedback.

Keeping It Simple

In order to appear more educated, some of us like to use difficult words in our writing. However, this does not always work well because then readers will have a hard time understanding our message. You need to be straightforward in your message so that the key points do not get clouded by difficult words. Before writing, you need to think about your goals and intended message. This way, you can focus on making your message clear and concise. Eliminate words that do not add any important information, and keep the ones that communicate efficiently.

Having Purpose in Your Writing

All communication serves a purpose; understanding this purpose before drafting written communication can help you to remain focused on the topic at hand and improve the clarity of the text. What message are you attempting to get across? You need to answer this question in advance. The message's goal must be straightforward and clear to everybody. Try to begin writing with the most important information and provide more detailed explanations of this message later in the text. By doing this, you can keep the readers focused on your intended message.

Accepting Constructive Criticism
When someone criticizes or gives feedback about your writing, do your best not to get offended or upset. It does not mean that you are not good at writing. Feedback can help you develop yourself, so instead, strive to be grateful for the opportunity to improve. You can ask the other person to elaborate on what aspects you need to improve. You may then use the feedback in your future writing.

Using Instant Messaging to Your Advantage

Instant messaging is definitely convenient, but these types of messages are often the most distracting, especially in groups. Don't forget that even though they are short messages, they should still be checked for errors and tone. Messages should still be professional. It is also a good idea to have policies in place for how to use your instant messaging software, and what is appropriate to send versus what is not. When IMs become distracting or the original message and point are lost, you should pick up the phone or have a face-to-face conversation, so as not to waste time. Let's take a look at the rules to apply when using instant messaging in a professional setting:
- **Keeping it professional:**
    - In a workplace, you need to always stay professional. No matter what tool you use to communicate, you have to keep the conversation respectful and polite. If the emojis you use are suitable for the people you

are communicating with, you can add them to make the message more engaging.

- **Giving your full attention:**

    - People want to interact more quickly and effectively at work. This is why they prefer to talk through instant messaging tools. When talking to someone through this tool, you need to do the other person the courtesy of giving them your attention and avoid getting distracted by other apps on your phone or computer.

- **Sticking to the subject:**

    - You need to stick to the topic that is intended from the start. Sometimes, it can be tempting to wander off the subject when talking to a coworker. However, you will waste time that could be used to finish your tasks. Stay on the subject, and you will be more effective and productive at work. If it is a serious personal matter that your coworker needs to discuss, then you can ask if they wish to discuss that matter with you now and offer to reschedule the original subject for a better, less stressful time.

- **Understanding the company's rules:**

    - Every company has its own sensitive information that should not be shared through unsafe tools. This is why you need to find what information or data you can deliver through instant messaging apps.

What You Need to Remember About Video Conferencing

These days, many companies choose to hold meetings through virtual communication. Video conferencing has developed into an essential for companies to manage their remote workers and settle business operations abroad. No matter where they are in the world, connecting people is the fundamental goal of virtual communication.

Attending a meeting can make us nervous, regardless of how we do it. Video conferencing might sound easy to some; for others, video calls may be harder to handle. Regardless of your personal philosophy when it comes to this form of communication, just as with face-to-face meetings, you need to prepare yourself before attending. Learning how to improve in virtual meetings is very important for leaders.

Preparing Your Space

There are some practical steps in preparing your work environment for a virtual meeting: The first is to ensure that the camera is positioned properly. The camera needs to be facing you directly and not to one side. This allows you to virtually make eye contact and build rapport with other members of the meeting. Another thing to pay attention to is the lighting; you need to prepare good lighting to ensure that you can be clearly seen throughout the meeting. You can turn on all the lights in the room or add an additional one like a ring light. Try to avoid backlighting, which can cast your face into a shadow. Instead, make sure that you are lit from the front or above.

Preparing Mentally and Physically

Before a virtual meeting, you also need to prepare yourself mentally and physically. Physically, you may want to move your body to make it feel relaxed and comfortable. You need to sit straight on your chair with your shoulders wide open. This will show that you are ready to listen during the meeting and confident in your work. Additionally, this posture helps you breathe properly and use your voice freely. Even though it is a virtual meeting, people can still see how you look, so you need to remember to act appropriately.

Mentally, you can visualize the meeting and the result you wish to accomplish in your head. When you do this, you will keep those goals in the front of your mind throughout the meeting. When you feel anxious and nervous, it might be hard to control your breathing. For this reason, it is best to practice deep breathing to regulate your nervous system prior to the meeting.

Effectively Challenging Others in Virtual Meetings

You can control the situation, maintain your composure, and contribute to asserting authority with your breath and voice. As female leaders, we may have a hard time staying silent during a difficult conversation. However, keep in mind to take a breath before talking so that you have time to gather your thoughts. Instead of spouting off an unprepared response when faced with a challenging situation, you need to prepare yourself in your mind first. This way, you will speak more calmly and your tone will sound more controlled.

Fortunately, virtual meetings make it more difficult for others to talk over you because turn-based conversation is reinforced by the limitations of the technology, and people not speaking often utilize the mute button, meaning they must pause to unmute before being able to speak. If someone interrupts, you can just tell them that you are speaking and you will give them a chance after that. Lastly, assert your authority with your voice. To keep the audience interested, you can change your tone of voice throughout the meeting. Also, always conclude sentences with a consistent tone of voice, which will turn them into statements rather than questions. What you say matters, so don't worry about what other people think; simply, aim to communicate your message clearly.

Overcoming Communication Barriers

Whenever you learn something, there will be obstacles that come your way. In communication, there are also barriers that you must face and overcome. When you can get past them, you will know how to share information in better ways while also understanding what you are being told by another person. Here is a list of actions that you can do to overcome communication barriers.

Actions to Overcome Communication Barriers	Checklist
Speaking with clarity, and explaining in terms that everyone can understand.	
Not elaborating upon more than one idea at a time.	
Respecting the other person's decision when they do not want to talk to you.	
Ensuring that the other person has understood what you said by asking questions.	
Talking in a place where there are no external interruptions.	
Recognizing any feelings the other person may have about what you said.	

Connecting with people's emotions is one area of leadership that can really set women apart. There are two key skills that enable leaders to connect with emotions, and although women are generally proficient in these areas, there is normally still room for improvement. We will discover what these skills are in the next chapter.

The Value of Support

"Support women on their way to the top. Trust that they will extend a hand to those who follow." – Mariela Dabbah

Remember Stephanie's story from the beginning of the book? Imagine how much different her experience might have been if the other female manager in the meeting with her had offered support rather than rolling her eyes.

It's true that she would most likely still have experienced imposter syndrome in that first meeting, and there's no getting around the fact that she was in a room full of men, where the risk of her ideas being dismissed was high. But if she'd had that support from her female colleague, she would probably have bounced back from that experience far quicker.

As women in the male-dominated world of business, the support we lend each other is crucial. It's not that we don't have the skills without it; the problem is that the world is set up to knock our confidence at every turn, and that support from fellow women can make all the difference to our self-esteem.

It's with this in mind that I'd like to ask for your help now. Half of our battle as women in business is recognizing that our struggles are real and we're not alone – and with just a few minutes of your time, you can remind other women of that, and point them in the direction of the guidance that will help them.

By leaving a review of this book on Amazon, you'll show other women that they're not the only ones facing these challenges, and you'll show them where they can find exactly what they need to build their confidence and move forward.

Scan to leave a review

Simply by letting other readers know how this book has helped you and what they can expect to find inside, you'll provide that much needed support to someone else – no matter how many people are rolling their eyes at them in the boardroom.

Thank you so much for your support. We're always stronger together and never is that more true than we're standing alone in front of a crowd, preparing to deliver a presentation.

5
The Part of Communication That Many Leaders Forget

"One of the criticisms I have faced over the years is that I'm not aggressive enough or assertive enough, or maybe somehow, because I'm empathetic, it means I'm weak. I totally rebel against that. I refuse to believe that you cannot be both compassionate and strong." – Jacinda Ardern

Here, we face one of the biggest biases in leadership, the idea that men are strong and assertive while women are overly concerned about emotions. It is the ability to be emotionally aware that enables women to excel in leadership. Aside from reading body language, this requires both listening and empathy.

What Does It Mean to Be an Active Listener?

As mentioned briefly in Chapter 2, active listening means being completely present in a conversation—whether face-to-face or virtual—observing all aspects of communication—not just word choice—and not being distracted by anything else, including mind-wandering. This includes the use of eye contact and other nonverbal communication as well as paying attention to nonverbal cues. Finally, active listening is about avoiding judgments.

Active listening is an essential part of communication. When we actively listen, the other person will feel heard and appreciated. In any environment, this ability is the basis of effective and successful communication. When we actively listen, it shows that we are focused and aware of what is going on around us. Let's take a look at the several benefits of active listening.

Resolving Conflicts

Through active listening, you can resolve conflicts and disagreements. You can better understand the other person's point of view and respond to it effectively by paying close attention to what they are saying and how they are saying it. By making your conversation partner feel respected and heard, you can also show them that there are flaws in their argument without risking them getting defensive. When they realize their own mistakes, they will back down and are willing to reach an agreement with you. In a professional negotiation, active listening allows you to analyze every aspect of a message so that you can obtain the best possible outcome from the other party. When conversation partners aren't listening to each other—or are overly focused on each other's phraseology—a compromise can almost never be reached. But through active listening, you can advance the conversation so that you can resolve the conflict or find a middle ground.

Establishing Trust

An advantage to be gained from active listening is that it can help you establish trust with the people around you. By developing trust, other people will feel safe disclosing information or knowledge to you, which can be helpful when seeking feedback or striving for agreement. As a leader, you must try to create and develop trust among your team members. When you can actively listen to them, your team will function more harmoniously and effectively. You have to be attentive to your team and watch out for any indications of withdrawal.

When your team members know how to actively listen, they can understand your point of view. In the same way, when you truly listen to your team, they will feel appreciated and respected. Simply put, active listening fosters trust and creates a powerful team.

Minimizing Mistakes
In any workplace, there are countless chances for mistakes to sneak in. When you actively listen and understand everything being said, you can better identify, handle, and resolve any potential problems. By making sure that important information is not overlooked, this skill can help you reduce mistakes. Active listening assists you in retaining information, which means that you can remember more details when you need them. This is essential when you have to learn new information or processes because you will not forget them easily. Moreover, this skill makes sure that you understand the intended message, and if you are confused, you will be empowered to ask questions for clarification knowing that you haven't simply missed something they said.

Developing Empathy and Compassion
In order to properly understand your team members, you need to have patience. Active listening helps you to grasp everything before jumping to conclusions or getting upset. Your team members might have a variety of emotions throughout the day. If you do not take the time to listen to them and comprehend their issues, their performance will suffer and they will make more mistakes. This means that you need to observe the personalities of all your team members and listen to their needs so that you can act accordingly. Active listening allows you to achieve this by making use of paralanguage

analysis to read more subtle communication clues that display emotions.

Enhancing Productivity

As a leader, you need to be attentive to your team members so that you can keep them productive. Those who feel heard are more content in their positions and are willing to advance their work as well as relationships in the workplace. People will look for employment prospects elsewhere if they do not feel listened to or respected by their leaders. In meetings, it is very easy for our minds to wander when in-depth information is being delivered. This is why active listening is crucial to stop your mind from straying away and prevent distractions. You can work on some questions you want to ask the speaker to keep your mind focused. When your team sees that you are engaged in what they are saying, they will feel more motivated to perform better at work.

Steps to Being a Better Listener

Sometimes, it takes effort to develop active listening skills. A lot of leaders think that active listening only means opening their ears to hear the other person, but it is more than that. As a leader who wants to be a better listener, here are some techniques you can follow and practice.

Establishing a Safe Environment

One crucial aspect of active listening is fostering an atmosphere in which people feel at ease discussing difficult or complicated subjects. To be a leader, you need to be someone that your team is comfortable talking to. If people are scared of you or do not trust you, there will be no communication at all. They will close themselves off from you or even talk about you behind your back. To be a better listener, you can implement an open communications policy that permits everyone to voice their ideas. You may inform your team members that your door is always open to those who want to share their opinions and that you are willing to listen to them with no judgments.

Asking Open-Ended Questions

You can understand any conversation topic better when you ask open-ended questions. These questions require an extended explanation in response—as opposed to a simple yes or no. They will show that you are paying attention and genuinely engaged in what they have to say. This may also encourage them to keep talking, which will give you more chances to listen. Before you ask the questions, however, you need to make sure that the other person has finished speaking. When it is your moment to speak, you should start by asking questions instead of offering answers.

If you are confused about something, you have to ask for clarification rather than making assumptions. This will expand your comprehension of the topic while also keeping you engaged throughout the discussion. Be curious, and if you disagree about something, you can provide feedback or constructive criticism after the other person has finished talking and offer clarifying responses to your questions.

Recognizing a Person's Emotions

People may become emotional when talking about some subjects, especially sensitive issues or those concerning confidential information. You need to recognize this as it happens and assure the other person that it is okay to have these feelings. If they need some time to gather their thoughts, give them their space. In a professional setting, your relationship with the team will be strengthened when you show kindness in difficult situations. This will help them trust and respect you more because you care about their feelings.

Eliminating Distractions

To actively listen, you need to clear any distractions around you. When in a conversation, remember to shut your books and put any documents away. If you have a computer in front of you, you can put it in sleep mode. If you have your phone around, try to keep it on silent mode so that you do not get distracted by any notifications. Distractions will cause your mind to wander away from what is being said. It can be difficult if you are busy and have to be on your phone all the time, but when you are distracted, the other person will feel disrespected. To be a good leader, you need to show your team that your mind is focused without distractions when listening to them.

Avoiding the Urge to Interrupt

To be a better listener, you need to avoid interrupting the other person. Keep in mind that you will have your own opportunity to talk after they finish with their part. If you cannot hear them clearly, you can ask them to talk louder or you may move closer. You can also remove any external noise so that the other person does not have to repeat what they have to say.

Your personal beliefs are something else to take into account when communicating with people. These beliefs may drive you to interrupt the other person. But just because you disagree with them, that does not mean that you have the right to interrupt them. Strive to put these beliefs away when another person is talking and express them respectfully when you are given the chance.

Using Nonverbal Cues and Eye Contact

To show that you are open to talking, you can make use of nonverbal communication. It's important for you to be comfortable with the situation and turn your body to face the other person so that you can focus on the discussion. You can also check their nonverbal cues to see if they are already comfortable or not. If not, you can help them become more relaxed by making a joke to lessen the tension.

Making eye contact is crucial when you are in a conversation. You don't have to stare at them all the time, but you need to check in with brief moments of eye contact from time to time to show the other person that you are engaged in the conversation. Making eye contact can be difficult if you are not used to it, but you can learn step by step.

Smiling More

No one feels comfortable around a person who always looks gloomy or angry. In a conversation, gently smiling will show that you are open to listening to the other person. When you do not smile, people will think that you are a cold person, which makes them reluctant to come to you or express an honest opinion. However, keep in mind that context is vital: You need to observe the situation before smiling and only do so if the subject is appropriate for a smile. When discussing a sensitive topic, you should not smile because it might send the wrong message.

Being Open-Minded

Being open-minded when listening means being prepared to not let what you hear negatively affect you in the moment. It does not mean that you should not have your own opinions on the topic, but you need to hear what other people have to say and understand their perspectives. Some people are not willing to listen to another opinion that does not match their own. When they listen to something they disagree with, they will argue to defend what they believe. However, this is not good for communication because you can never find a middle ground. Whenever you have to talk to someone, it's crucial to keep your mind open and accept that everyone has their own beliefs. You can show your views without forcing others to follow what you believe.

Not Forcing Your Opinions or Giving Unsolicited Advice

Sometimes, listening and giving moral support to someone is enough. You should never force someone to accept your opinions or give them advice when they haven't even asked for it. If someone comes to you with their problems, your gut instinct may be to help them to solve their issues and give them solutions. However, this is not always a good idea because they might not even want them. You cannot tell someone what to do if they are not willing to accept it. People sometimes choose to find their own answers without others' help. Instead, what they are often seeking, by bringing up an issue in conversation, is empathy. The next time someone comes to you to talk, just be there for them to listen to and support them.

What Happens When a Team Has an Empathetic Leader?

Leadership is not about being in charge. Leadership is about taking care of those in your charge. –Simon Sinek

Empathetic leadership centers around building relationships with your team members and appreciating as well as valuing their perspectives. This approach helps you in understanding your team's personal ideas, emotions, and views. Becoming an empathetic leader involves making an effort to learn about your team members' motivations. As a result, you can build and maximize their potential. Additionally, you will make sure that everyone feels listened to when they deal with difficulties. Here are a few advantages of becoming an empathetic leader:

- Encourages team collaboration:
    - When you become an empathetic leader, you will encourage your team members to work together and collaborate. When there is a project, you will assist your team to solve the problems that arise. When the team encounters any issues, you are also there with them for support. Empathy enhances collaboration when you involve your team in making important decisions. When the work environment is supportive, your team will feel a sense of belonging and be happy to work with you.

- Fosters better relationships:
    - Being empathetic means that you can connect with your team more easily. When you have better connections with each other, you will feel more comfortable working together because you can communicate your issues. You can try to be more empathetic by asking how your team is feeling and offering compassionate responses. Perhaps, you can even ask them appropriate personal questions to express your care, which might deepen your relationships.

- Promotes productivity:
    - Your team will become self-aware when you are empathetic toward them. Your team members will be able to support and connect with one another because they know what their responsibilities are at the company. As an empathetic leader, you create a secure, reliable, and empowering environment so that your team can concentrate on their work and become more productive.

- Creates a healthy work-life balance:
    - As an empathetic leader, you will not overwork your

team members. This means that your team will have time to spend with their loved ones outside of work. They will also become happier because they won't have to think about work all the time, even at home. Many leaders think that they can improve their team's performance by raising work hours, but this is not true because people need rest and vacation too to avoid burnout.

- Develops creativity:
  - Because empathetic leaders create a supportive environment, their team will be more creative as well. Your team will feel heard whenever they talk, and when they have new ideas, they will feel comfortable expressing them to you. This motivates your team members to contribute, think creatively, and face new challenges to prove themselves to you.

How to Be an Empathetic Yet Strong Female Leader

Remember that being empathetic is not the same as being overly sensitive or too emotional. First and foremost, it is about developing your own emotional awareness and learning how to recognize emotions in others.

When you are leading a team, you become their role model and they follow whatever you do. If you communicate empathetically with them, they will follow your lead and do the same.

If a team member comes to you to talk about an issue, you should treat them with care and tell them that you understand their feelings. Actively listening to what they say will make sure that you understand their perspective before sharing your own opinions or making assumptions.

Before being able to practice empathy in your team, you need to make sure you are not feeling overwhelmed or stressed out at work. When you are in a bad position mentally and emotionally, your own circumstances obfuscate your empathy skills. An overwhelmed leader can never understand a team and their issues.

Emotional intelligence is also essential if you want to become an empathetic and strong leader. When you are emotionally intelligent, you become more aware of your feelings. When you recognize your emotions as they appear, you can be better at communicating with others. You become capable of controlling your emotions without exploding if you have emotional intelligence. This is important when you are a leader because emotional intelligence will allow you to resolve issues and communicate objectively without taking things too personally. You can also present yourself as a reliable figure to your team because your emotions will not get in the way of work.

With emotional intelligence, you will be able to read people's feelings and the situations around you. This means that you can respond to problems properly and communicate with the people involved to reach an agreement. You will not act impulsively because you think things through and assess the situation carefully before making a decision. As a leader, you need to create a productive and comfortable working environment for your team. When you know how to resolve issues and find successful solutions, your team members will be happier working for you.

Practices to Become an Empathetic Leader

When you are an empathetic leader, you make your team feel valued and safe around you. This is because you are compassionate and you care for your team. Being empathetic also makes you more trusted even in times of anxiety and stress. Here are some techniques you may use to develop your empathy as a leader.

You need to be willing to assist your team with personal matters. Many leaders believe that their team members have to leave their personal issues at home when they go to work. It is challenging to achieve this if your team feels so much pressure and stress from their personal lives. With no one to listen to or help them, these issues will hinder their productivity at work. Try to understand that everyone has their own lives and problems, and you cannot just ignore them. Work to be your team's support system because you are their leader. Showing them that you care about them and are willing to help them as best as you can will, in and of itself, ease some of their stress and, in turn, improve their productivity. Open your doors to your team at all times, and show them that they can come to you whenever they have issues at home or at work. Oftentimes, your team members just need someone to talk to, so when you are open, they will feel more comfortable with you.

Another practice is to display interest in your team members and their situations. As an empathetic leader, you must realize that everyone has their experiences in life, which means they will have their own unique life circumstances. When you understand this, you can delegate tasks according to what they are good at or have the mental capacity for day to day. When the tasks fit your team members perfectly, you will boost their productivity and satisfaction levels at work. Your team will also see that you are concerned with their needs and situations, which will make them more motivated because you are willing to go above and beyond for them.

You may also plan one-on-one conversations with your team members. As an empathetic person, you need to understand everyone's emotions. To find out how they are feeling, you can meet them one at a time. If you do not have time to plan all the meetings, you can ask your team members to let you know when they are free and match these periods with your own schedule. It is impossible to understand everybody just by observing them; it helps for you to talk to your team members about their lives and situations. These meetings don't even have to take place at the office, you can talk them over lunch or coffee.

Furthermore, it is vital to pay attention to work burnout. Workplace burnout is a severe problem, and it becomes even more of an issue when your team members are under a lot of stress. Burnout can be very harmful and widespread if not treated immediately and effectively. Even when your team members are working on a tight deadline, time *must* be made for rejuvenation or they will not be productive. Being an empathetic leader is important here because you will be able to spot the symptoms of burnout earlier and resolve them immediately.

Becoming a Good Leader

To become a good leader for your team, you need to be self-aware. Before you can improve yourself, you must assess your self-awareness levels and skills. You can rate your skills on a scale from one to five and calculate your overall score to determine how effectively you can apply self-awareness. If there is a particular area of self-awareness that you struggle with, don't panic, you can improve with a little bit of effort.

Self-Awareness Skills	Scale				
	1	2	3	4	5
Having empathy					
Staying focused					
Being mindful					
Setting boundaries					
Understanding your emotional triggers					
Apologizing when you make a mistake					
Asking for feedback					
Having an open mind					
Practicing self-discipline					
Being patient					
Adapting to new situations					
Having self-confidence					
Being kind toward others					

In a perfect world, we would all have outstanding role models in our workplace—women we could look up to and admire. Considering, however, that just 8.8% of Fortune 500 companies have women in leadership positions and that only 35% of top management positions are held by women, it is a challenge to find inspirational examples to learn from (Ariella, 2022). Nevertheless, networking is an essential skill that can take you further in your career.

Networking Like a Queen Bee

"If you want to go fast, go alone. If you want to go far, go with others." – African Proverb

If we want to see the change with our workplaces, and if we want to *be* the change within our communities, the only way to do this is with others!

The Difference Between Mentors and Sponsors

It takes work to build a successful and fulfilling career, and it is ineffective and more difficult to try to do it alone. Without the assistance of others, it can be challenging to gain insight or clarity when making crucial decisions in your career. Finding prospects to advance your career can be very difficult if your potential has not been recognized by those in power. You cannot expect to be noticed based on your skills alone. This is why you need to have mentors and sponsors so that you can advance and become a leader in your workplace. But how are a mentor and a sponsor different from one another?

Mentors are people with experience in the field who can offer advice and guidance. Typically, when you have a mentor, it means that they work in the same industry as you. They might have even held positions or roles similar to yours. This means that they will serve as an example that you want to follow. Because they have been through your position, you can ask them career-related questions in different circumstances. Your mentor can also assist you in discovering your own future vision for your career advancement. Your mentor probably had the same goals as you, and they have accomplished them, which means that they can let you know what directions to take and what decisions to make.

A sponsor differs from a mentor because they will advocate for you, help you advance your career, and put you up for promotions. A sponsor will proactively add you to their network of connections. We like to think that as long as we have the skills or our performance is good, we can advance. However, this is not always the case because companies typically trust the word of an established sponsor over the work of an unsponsored employee. Because of this, sponsors are generally people with leadership roles—leaders who recognize the potential in you and want you to achieve success with their help.

These days, many companies open up workplace sponsorship programs that pair young professionals with powerful leaders who may assist them in their career development. This is an important move for those who have historically been underrepresented, such as women and other minority groups. According to research, women are 24% less likely to get advice from senior leaders than men, and 62% of women of color feel they are at a disadvantage because they do not have an influential mentor (Sokolowsky, 2022).

How to Find a Mentor

As explained above, having a mentor can help you advance your career. A mentor is someone you can rely on when you have questions and problems about your work. They will give you advice and guidance so that you can stick to the right path for your career advancement. Let's take a look at how you can find yourself a mentor.

The first step is to not be scared to ask. Some of us may be reluctant to ask someone to be our mentor for fear that we might get rejected. You can't do everything by yourself if you wish to advance your position because you need someone to guide you in the right direction. You don't have to know everything before asking someone to be your mentor. Show them that you are willing to learn and that you know what it takes to accomplish what you want. You deserve and are qualified to advance, and your mentor can assist you with it.

Let's say that you see how skilled your coworker is at resolving an issue for a project. You should tell them about your observations and explain how impressed you are. If you want them to mentor you, don't be hesitant to ask. However, you need to be specific about what you are likely to need from them. Perhaps, you require some guidance about a problem you are facing. Maybe, you wish to learn a new skill that they are good at. Whatever it is, you have to be clear and unafraid of asking.

It is also helpful to look for opportunities to expand your network. You can become more confident when you have the knowledge and experience in what you are doing. To find a mentor, you can seek out new opportunities outside your workplace. For instance, when you have the chance to attend a conference, that would be an excellent opportunity to talk to different people and grow your network. By doing this, you might find someone that can become a good mentor for you. Find out their name and what they do. After that, you can reach out to them in person or online. You can also search for and connect with a mentor on LinkedIn. You can then contact them if you have any questions about your career.

How to Find a Sponsor

You have learned that a sponsor is someone who can also help you advance your career because they will advocate for you and your success. They will also spread your name so that you can be recognized by the higher-ups. Let's explore some ways you can gain sponsorship.

First, you must work hard and establish your worth. When you begin a new position, you may want to find a sponsor right away. However, this might be harder because you have not established yourself in your position yet. You have to put in some effort to gain success and several recognizable achievements to enable potential sponsors to see your worth. In order to gain sponsorship, you must have a good reputation at your workplace because a sponsor will risk theirs for you. Your sponsor will spread your name, but you will also need to prove yourself through your work.

A sponsor is always a supportive person. Therefore, look for people who go above and beyond to encourage and uplift others. If you see someone who likes to compliment the people around them, you can be sure that they are a supportive person. However, if they enjoy yelling or shouting at others, they might not be a good fit to be your sponsor. Somebody in your workplace who publicly supports others is probably also willing to do the same in private. Potential sponsors are usually excellent listeners and good at building relationships with people.

Before asking someone to sponsor you, you need to verify if they really can do so. A good sponsor will have the time and flexibility to advocate for you. You should not ask someone with an extremely busy schedule because they probably can't provide you with sufficient time and guidance. If you see someone who has sponsored others and you are interested in asking them, you have to make sure that they can support you the same way. You need someone who can be available to advocate for you and your advancement.

Additionally, you have to specify what you want from your sponsor. You need to define your goals before you can ask someone to sponsor you. This will allow you to be clear and honest about what you need from them. Perhaps, you want them to help you get promoted or to expand your network to include more powerful people. You need to also ask them how you are going to communicate—maybe, one phone call every month or a face-to-face meeting every few months. Be clear about your expectations so that the sponsor can take care of their schedule as well.

Once you find someone who meets the requirements for a sponsor, you can begin to communicate with them. This can be done in a face-to-face meeting or via email. Perhaps, you could take them out for coffee or lunch or even ask them to join you in a private *Zoom* meeting. You need to be clear and direct about what you are looking for, rather than dragging out the conversation for too long, because they might be busy. You can tell them you would like to advance your career and expand your network with their help and ask if they are willing to assist you in your journey. If this first discussion goes well, you can ask them when they are free to schedule a time to talk again and establish a stronger relationship.

How to Succeed at Networking Events

When trying to advance your career, it's important to connect with new people and expand your network whenever you have the opportunity. These days, many professionals choose to attend networking events to make it easier to build their con-

nections with others. It can be difficult to navigate in-person networking when you are not used to it. The following are some tips to follow so that you can be prepared when attending a networking event:
- **Network prior to looking for a job:**
    - We all have applied for jobs, and we know how difficult the process is. However, having someone to contact can make a huge difference. This is why you need to start networking before engaging in a job search to make it simpler. When you need a job, you can then reach out to one of your acquaintances and ask if they know of any job openings. By doing this, you will be one step ahead of other job seekers.
- **Have a goal:**
    - The next time you attend a networking event, you need to prepare and plan. What are your goals? Maybe, you want to meet certain people from specific companies. Some events will share a list of attendees ahead of time, so you can check that out first. It will be easier to maintain your attention during the event when you have a clear objective from the start. When you have no goal, you cannot converse well with others.
- **Introduce yourself to experienced people:**
    - Oftentimes, we attend networking events because we want to meet important people, such as a CEO or a writer that we admire. Since you'll be excited to have a chance to meet them, when you see them in person, you might become nervous or anxious. In order to successfully approach them, you should not act like a fan but as an equal. You can introduce yourself and compliment their work while also relating your experiences to what they do. This way, you have the chance to respect and admire them

while they can simultaneously be impressed with your work as well.

- **Ask questions about the other person:**

    ○ Normally, when you meet someone at a networking event, you just ask them about basic things like what their job is, where they work, or where they come from. After that, you might not know what else to talk about. To solve this, you have to show a genuine interest in the other person. For instance, if you meet a writer, you can ask them if they are planning to write a new book in the future. If they do, you can expand your questions about the book. By doing this, the conversation can keep going without getting awkward.

- **Listen actively:**

    ○ The most important thing to keep in mind when talking with someone at a networking event is to actively listen. Some of us might be so excited about what we do that we end up simply sharing what we want without considering the other person. When you want to establish a connection with people, you need to show that you are interested in them and listen to what they have to say. You may ask questions or rephrase what they say to demonstrate that you are paying attention to the conversation.

- **Bring a notebook:**

    ○ To ensure that you remember everyone you talk to at an event, you need to make notes. Sometimes, we might forget things if we interact with so many people. When you have a meaningful discussion with someone, you can write down their details and keep in touch with them later on. This will also make you look very professional and help you to gain respect.

- **Ask for what you want:**
  - As mentioned before, you need to prepare your goals for attending an event. This means that if you want to achieve something, you need to ask for it. For instance, if you want to land a client, you need to be straightforward with the other person. However, you should do so politely. Try complimenting their work first, and then, express your wish. When you make a clear request with confidence, you can impress others.

- **Keep in touch:**
  - A networking event helps you meet other people from different fields and companies that you can connect to. However, this will not turn into a relationship if you do not keep in touch with them. This is why it is best practice to drop them a message or email in the first 24 hours after talking to them. Perhaps, you could even ask them to meet in person for coffee.

Conversation Topics That Will Make You Stand Out

In a conversation, there are some things that are and aren't acceptable. By remaining cognizant of these things, you will be able to connect with the other person and become more comfortable with each other. For instance, it is generally helpful to ask open-ended questions, make eye contact, smile, discuss a topic that interests you, pay close attention to the other person, and listen to them. It is also very beneficial for networking if you use the other person's name in the conversation, ask for their opinion on a topic, and offer help if they need your assistance.

On the other hand, interrupting when the other person is talking, asking a closed yes-or-no question, telling an offensive joke, talking about yourself too much, gossiping about other people, and getting angry when a conversation doesn't go your way are all best avoided. When you can remember all these dos and don'ts, you will become better at connecting with people.

Questions for Networking Events

At a networking event, you meet new people that you can establish relationships or partnerships with. This means you have to talk and create meaningful conversations with them. If you have no idea what topics to talk about, you can learn some questions to use as conversation starters. According to Jennifer Herrity (2022), there are a couple of basic questions you may use to begin and maintain conversations:

- Hello, my name is (name), and I work for (company). What do you do?

- What is your top networking advice for introverted people?

- You appear to be enjoying yourself a lot. May I accompany you?

- Have you checked out the food stands? I heard they are nice.

- The speech was excellent, wasn't it? What message did you get from it?

- Do you maybe know of a nice restaurant in this area?

- Where did you come in from? Are you local to the area?

- What is your opinion on the décor of this venue today?
- Are you interested in making a speech at a networking event in the future?
- Which skill are you interested in mastering?
- What do you enjoy most about working in your position?
- What do you enjoy doing when you have some time for yourself? Do you have any hobbies?
- What is your favorite book? And what are you currently reading?
- Why are you here at this networking event? Do you have any goals in mind?

Questions to Establish Meaningful Conversations
If you want to create more meaningful conversations, there are some topics you can present in conversation that will help people open up to you. Here are some conversation starters you could use to connect with the other person on a deeper level:
- Technology is advancing so quickly! In 10 years, what do you envision life will be like?
- People are switching positions rapidly now. Are you happy with your position?
- Which element of your job offers you the most happiness and satisfaction?
- I love how people are challenging the status-quo for self-exploration. What does success look like to you now?
- Are you someone who prefers to take risks or go with the flow?

- What is the top priority in your professional life right now?

- What is your dream career?

- What has been your fondest memory of working at your company?

Ending Conversations Gracefully

First impressions count, but so do our final impressions. Not knowing how to end a conversation can lead to awkward moments. It can also lead to getting stuck in a conversation for fear of seeming rude, but this has knock-on effects as you are missing out on creating other potential connections, and the goal of any networking event is to make as many new connections as possible. If you are unsure how to exit a conversation politely, the following are some tips you may consider:
- **Proposing that you get in touch later:**
    - If you really like talking to the other person but have an urgent matter to attend to, you can ask them to speak again later before the event ends or offer to meet them for coffee another day.

- **Turning your attention elsewhere:**
    - If you want to stop talking to someone, you can say that you see someone you know or that you want to meet other people at the event.

- **Waiting for a pause:**
  - There will be pauses that happen during a conversation. When this occurs, you can excuse yourself politely and tell them it was great talking to them.

- **Scheduling a follow-up:**
  - If you discover a meaningful and helpful connection, you can ask them if they want to keep in touch. You can request their contact information, like a phone number or email, so that you can continue the conversation later on.

- **Grabbing more drinks or food:**
  - There are typically food stands available at a networking event. If you are unsure how to leave a conversation, you may just say that you need to get more drinks or food.

- **Inviting a new person into the conversation:**
  - If you see someone you know at the event, you can introduce them to the other person. After they get into the conversation, you can excuse yourself and let them talk.

Setting the Example and Creating Networking Events

You do not have to be an owner of a company to create a networking event. You can take the initiative and set an example for other professional women yourself. The first thing you need to do is establish clear goals for what you wish the network to accomplish. It can be helpful to ask yourself if you want the new network to be motivated by a certain topic or field of interest. After deciding this, you will need to draft a document that outlines the network's mission statement and that everybody who will eventually attend the networking event will agree to—for instance, "Network members will be given the chance to learn from one another and outside experts."

After that, you need to organize the network. You can create a committee that oversees the network and consists of representatives from various fields. This can be achieved by establishing a process to join the committee and opening applications to enter. You may then delegate tasks to the committee members, whether it be assisting with event management or giving presentations. Scheduling meetings with the committee will ensure that there is open communication about the network and progress in organizing the event.

In addition, your committee will aim to recruit people with different skills to join the network. For this reason, it can be advantageous, when people join, give them a list of questions to answer about the reason they want to be a member, what they wish to contribute, and how much time they will devote to the network. This way, you will know what skills the members have and be able to utilize them to expand the network even more.

Moreover, you have to draw attention to the network. Consider how the network will develop in the long run: How will you promote the network so that it can be recognized at your company or outside? You need to make sure that the network is beneficial to its members and becomes successful so that it can get noticed by other people.

Lastly, you need to use the virtual world to its full potential. A lot of us have been working from home since the COVID-19 outbreak. As a result, you should also create virtual networking events. You can make these entertaining and interesting by inviting an expert to speak and letting people talk to each other by creating a group on *WhatsApp* or *Slack*. You can also explore an interesting topic for each networking event and change it at every event.

The Best Places to Network

If you want, you can network anywhere you wish. Networking does not only happen at work events because you may do it everywhere. You should bring your business cards wherever you go because you might get a chance to meet unexpected people who can help you advance your career. Here are some places you can consider to network:

- **Cultural events:**
    - These can be art exhibitions, yearly Renaissance fairs, or museum events.
- **Volunteer events:**
    - You can volunteer at a food bank, homeless shelter, or church event.
- **Health clubs:**
    - You may talk to people at yoga classes or gym sessions.

- **Outdoor activities:**
    - These can happen when you are out hiking or taking a walk in the park.

- **Parties:**
    - You can network with people through office parties, supper clubs, or even birthday parties.

- **Coffee shops:**
    - Many people work and hang out at coffee shops, and if you see that someone is friendly and conversational, you could learn more about what they do.

- **Friends and family:**
    - Your loved ones might know people that they can connect you to.

- **Alumni events:**
    - You can keep in touch with your old friends from high school or college.

Before dealing with really difficult workplace issues, we are going to take advantage of the next chapter to discover what it takes to become an assertive communicator and deal with common conflicts that arise in the workplace.

Assertive Communication and Conflict Resolution

"Don't call me bossy. If I were a boy, you'd call me a leader. To the women who are labeled bossy, keep leading. To the women who are labeled aggressive, keep being assertive. To the women who are labeled difficult, keep telling the truth. Gender bias is real, and the language we use is important." – The Female Lead

Take a brief moment to recognize that gender bias comes from both genders. When a person of any gender uses terms like "she's the Angry Black Woman" or "she must be hormonal today," we are fueling stereotypes not encouraging diversity.

How Can Women Master the Communication Balance?

In Chapter 3, we discussed how an assertive communication style is the best one for a leader to have. This style helps you express yourself better and stand firm on your perspective while also respecting and valuing the other person's viewpoint. By being assertive, you can be more confident and reduce your stress because you understand how to communicate and resolve problems. As female leaders, let's learn how to be better at assertive communication.

We have to express our viewpoints and be direct. Being assertive means that you need to express yourself clearly and without holding back or making excuses. You need to be direct about what you want while still showing respect for other people.

As a woman, you must be aware of your rights and know that you deserve them. Women are equal to men, so we do not have to hide away in the back corners of meeting rooms simply taking notes. Indeed, though there is still discrimination to this day, we not only deserve to share our thoughts confidently, but it is also our right.

We must also aim to take accountability when we make mistakes. Being assertive involves standing up for your opinions, but you also have to take responsibility if they are wrong. For instance, if your advice for a project turns out to be misguided and slows down progress, you need to apologize for this instead of blaming other people. This does not, however, mean taking blame for others' mistakes; they too should be held accountable for what they say or do.

If you have a hard time expressing your thoughts, you should practice what you want to say at home first. It can be helpful to prepare explanations for common scenarios that you may experience and practice saying them aloud. You may also write things down and read them aloud. When you actually have to face and talk to people, you will be more comfortable in the knowledge that you are prepared.

Moreover, preparing what to say can help you to process difficult emotions and express them appropriately. In the face of conflicts, it is often difficult to keep our feelings in check. You might feel furious, upset, or even cry. It is normal to have these emotions, but we should process them in private because becoming overwhelmed by emotion in the midst of a conversation will hinder us from resolving the conflict. If you feel emotional when there is an issue, you need to step back, take time to breathe, and calm your nerves before you can find a solution. It is okay to express, "I need a moment to think. Let's come back to this in 10 minutes."

Another aspect to consider is that women often use weak or subtle language that makes it seem as though they are not sure about what they want. For instance, you might have said, "I feel like this could be a good idea" in place of "Based on the research conducted, this is the strongest idea for us to follow through with." The structure of the prior statement—while often used as a method of politeness—shows that you are not confident and not convinced about the idea or your own opinion. The latter statement, on the other hand, shows conviction and a determination to take action, both of which will serve to bolster the respect your colleagues have for you. As a female leader, you need to avoid uncertain language to show self-confidence.

Last but not least, you avoid aggression. Many people think being assertive and being aggressive are the same thing, but as we learned in Chapter 3, they are not. When trying to be more assertive, you have to be careful not to go overboard. Being aggressive will cause resentment to build in other people, and they will lose respect for you.

Setting Boundaries Within Your Team

Without boundaries, other people have the power to treat you as they see fit. Ignoring known boundaries is a sign of disrespect. As a leader, you want your team to respect you, and this is why you must set and reinforce boundaries within your workplace. Let's take a look at some examples of how you can set healthy boundaries with your team:

- **Protect your space:**
    - This means that when you close your door for privacy, communicate beforehand that no one should come in unless it's an emergency. Virtually, you can set your profile to "Do Not Disturb" and add a public focus time slot to your work calendar.

- **Only accept politeness:**
    - In the team, you can tell them to always use polite words when talking to you. This should be the standard because you are in a professional and formal setting. Any rudeness should be followed up with appropriate consequences.

- **Establish your priorities:**
    - This involves communicating with your team your schedule and workload. No one can force you to help them or work on what they want because you have planned your day accordingly.

- **Put in place a strict policy against office gossip:**
    - You need to tell your team not to talk behind anyone's back. If they have a personal issue with you or other people, they need to first address it privately and directly. If it continues, then provide a safe place to discuss the issue and, if needed, connect

your team member to Human Resources to document the continuous concern.

Ways to Start Setting Up Boundaries

Your days at work will be much better when you can establish boundaries for yourself and decide what behaviors you will and won't tolerate from others. As a leader, you cannot always be liked because you are in a position of authority. Instead, you have to educate your team on how to treat you and behave around you. If you fail to establish boundaries, people will then treat you however they want, and this leaves a door open for much conflict.

The first step toward healthy personal boundaries is to know that you have the right to establish them. As women, we all have been told to "act like a lady" umpteen times. We've been told that we need to behave in certain ways and act feminine because of society's expectations for women. Subconsciously, many of us still follow what we are told, and even now, as adults, we have no idea how to break out from these restrictive rules. But no matter what you have been led to believe, you have the right to shift your personal values and set boundaries accordingly.

You need to also make a decision regarding what you can accept and what you cannot. This is a problem that many female leaders have encountered. We often think we don't have boundary issues. However, when we look back to our past experiences, we often see patterns of people-pleasing and demureness that we have simply accepted as normal. At work, however, we must break away from these narrow gender roles. You have to observe when you are constantly interrupted, dismissed, or ignored and make it very clear that this will not be accepted in the future. When these instances next occur, you need to state your boundaries and ask others to respect them.

It is important to consistently set your boundaries in practice. You must take appropriate action after deciding what you can and cannot accept in the workplace. You need to begin with little steps. To test how it feels, you can try implementing a boundary every week. If you make a mistake, don't despair; it is simply a learning opportunity, and you can use that mistake to inform future adjustments to how you set and reinforce your boundaries.

The Art of Delegating Without Nagging

As much as you want to do everything yourself—and while it might seem quicker in the short term—it doesn't give team members a chance to develop their skills or prove their abilities. Moreover, it is likely to leave you burned out from trying to do too much. Delegating tasks gives your team opportunities to feel empowered. At the same time, it allows all of you to thrive with a more balanced workload. However, it is also important to know how to delegate tasks without that delegation devolving into nagging. Let's explore some questions you can answer to guide you toward becoming better at delegating:

- *What are the tasks that only I can complete?*
    - This is when you need to take a look at your skills and expertise. By doing this, you will know how to determine tasks that require your specific focus and the ones that can be done by your team members. You may then delegate the tasks that your team can manage so that you have more time to concentrate on those that only you can do.

- *How important is this task?*
    - You need to determine the reason why the task

needs to be done and how urgently it must be completed. After that, you can choose the best team member to manage it without your assistance. This also means that you need to observe the skills of everyone in your team to make a decision.

- **What result do I want?**
    - When you know what result you want from every task, you will know its importance. This means that you will feel more secure when assigning it to a team member, knowing that you can clearly communicate your expectations and desired outcomes.

- **Why do I refuse to assign the task to a team member?**
    - Maybe, you feel like they will think that you are asking for too much, or perhaps, you fear that they won't be able to do it perfectly. You must find out the reasons why you do not want to delegate tasks so that you can discover a solution. Perhaps, you have to adjust your perspective, adopt a new mindset, learn to more clearly communicate the task briefing, and understand the benefits of task delegation for yourself and your team.

Giving and Receiving Constructive Criticism

Your career advancement depends heavily on getting constructive criticism. However, women and those from minority groups are less likely to receive feedback because of the workplace phenomenon known as *protective hesitation*. Protective hesitation happens when leaders refuse to have these potentially difficult conversations for fear of coming across as sexist, racist, ableist, or homophobic to their team members (Connley, 2022). However, as a leader, you need to be transparent and honest about your team's performance so that they can improve themselves. Feedback is not a bad thing because it can help people in their career advancement. Don't be scared of giving feedback just because your team members are part of a minority group. They also deserve to know where they can improve on their career journey so that they may get better positions in the future.

Moreover, leaders need to be able to receive feedback as well. When someone gives you constructive criticism, you should not get offended. This is the time when you can improve your performance as a leader. Open your door and your heart, so your team can meet you and talk about what they like and don't like about your leadership style. You may ask them to elaborate on anything and even question what they might do if they were in your position. If you disagree with them, you can explain your side and find a mutual understanding. If you realize that your way is wrong, you need to start making changes for the benefit of your team.

How to Give Feedback

Giving feedback to your team members can be difficult because there is a chance that it will hinder their progress or lower their confidence in their work. However, when you fail to give feedback, you can badly harm the performance of your team. The following are some ways to give more helpful and thoughtful feedback:

- **Choose a suitable environment:**
    - You need to pick a place that is quiet, private, and has no unnecessary distractions that can derail your conversation.

- **Be respectful:**
  - Being polite in giving someone feedback will reduce the risk of defensiveness on their part. You should never judge them and need to always consider their feelings.
- **Be specific:**
  - Giving specific feedback, with examples, to your team members will ensure that they can find solutions to improve more easily.
- **Prevent surprises:**
  - Try to conduct evaluations consistently and on a regular basis so that your team can prepare themselves before receiving feedback from you.
- **Stay relevant:**
  - You have to prioritize the truly crucial elements of your team member's performance while avoiding ambiguity that hinders their progress. Try not to move from one topic to another which will make them confused.

How to Receive Feedback

I know that not everybody responds well to criticism, but as a leader, you should. As long as the feedback is helpful and constructive, you must accept it and change your ways. Try not to react hastily and negatively when receiving feedback because this will prevent you from receiving opportunities for growth in the future. These are the essentials for receiving criticism:

- **Not taking it personally:**
  - When someone gives you feedback, try not to take

it personally. Your team is there to support you, so their feedback is most likely well-intended and not a personal attack on you.

- **Considering it a chance to improve:**
    - You need to put the feedback into practice so that you can be a better leader for your team.

- **Being self-aware:**
    - You must be aware of what will happen when you become emotional. Notice your own internal reactions when someone is giving you feedback and allow that to inform future self-work.

- **Asking for the basis for the criticism:**
    - Not every piece of feedback is fair; it might be unjustified or inappropriate. Asking the other person for more details and examples of the reason why they are criticizing you will allow you to evaluate how seriously the feedback should be taken. You may also ask other people if they feel the same way.

- **Requesting time and space to process the criticism:**
    - Before responding, you may ask for some time alone to process the feedback. This will help prevent you from lashing out or getting angry at the other person.

How to Resolve Conflicts Collaboratively

It is hard to imagine a workplace with absolutely no conflicts. There are different personalities, perceptions, and ideas mixed together. Poor communication and unclear work roles lead to misunderstandings, and if there is pressure to meet tight deadlines, tension may rise. While conflict is normal, ignoring it can lead to a cycle of negativity. As a leader, you must know how to resolve conflicts effectively.

To resolve conflicts effectively, first find a neutral location. A neutral space will encourage everyone involved to be constructive with their criticism. This will also help you create a sense of fairness in everyone's mind. The chosen space should make everybody comfortable so that they can talk about their issue more efficiently. If the meeting is virtual, be mindful of different time zones. Do your best to relieve as much discomfort as possible from this open discussion.

As a leader, you need to encourage fairness. To do this, you can establish ground rules that everyone must follow. This will make the discussion respectful and fair. It is best to allow everybody involved to be part of deciding on the ground rules as well, as this will encourage all individuals to adhere to them. For example, if your team has voiced, "I don't like being interrupted while I'm speaking," or "please don't insult my ideas if you don't agree with them," and as a result, you have forbidden unnecessary interruptions and rude insults toward each other when talking, the individuals who voiced the concerns are more likely to also monitor their own speech and adhere to this rule as they will not want to appear hypocritical. Whatever rules are decided on, the main goal is to keep things professional, formal, and collaborative so that no one takes things too personally.

Before the discussion, remind everyone to keep an open mind and not interrupt when someone else is talking. They need to listen to each other so that they can understand every side. During the discussion, you can mediate effectively by allowing everyone to share their opinions on the issue. As a leader, you need to guarantee that everyone has sufficient time to say their piece. After that, the other party can say what they want and make clear the differences in opinion so that the conflict can be solved.

Some leaders might think that all they need to do is give out solutions so that everyone can move on. But as a good leader, you should avoid doing this because it will make your team too dependent on you. Rather, you need to provide direction that aids your team members in discovering common ground and resolving their own conflicts. No one knows more about the issue at hand than the parties involved, so they should be the ones to find solutions. When they can make an agreement among themselves, they will get along better in the future.

Negotiating What You Deserve

Interestingly, men and women are equally likely to negotiate on behalf of a client or with a supplier. A gender difference is only seen when people need to negotiate for themselves. For example, men are more comfortable asking for a promotion, even if they have only met some of the requirements, whereas women are more inclined to see a promotion as a reward. The following are some ways to help you negotiate through challenging situations.

Preparation is the first step to effective negotiating. This involves collecting and processing information about the topic and the other party. This also calls for an understanding of the other party's needs, hopes, and concerns. To achieve clarity about the negotiation, you must gather enough information to be ready to ask and answer questions during the discussion. You can navigate the process better when you come prepared with all the necessary information.

You also should never rush the negotiation. It takes time to negotiate, particularly if you want the outcome to be positive for you. Spend some time developing an honest rapport with the other party. You can give some information about yourself to show that you are open, transparent, and eager to connect with them. By doing this, you can turn the negotiation battlefield into a positive environment for discussion. During the conversation, you may also create pauses so that everyone can think clearly and process any questionable emotions.

If the negotiation directly impacts you, it is easy to get emotional during the negotiation. However, being overly emotional will not help you here. You should try not to get offended because all you want is to achieve the best deal. Unlike with team-based communications—wherein a certain amount of vulnerability can help to build trust—showing your emotions during a negotiation should be avoided, where possible, because they might be used against you.

Additionally, you should never accept a bad deal. The process of negotiating can be dragged out, exhausting, and difficult. Perhaps, all you want is to end the process so that you can relax. Nevertheless, it is critical to keep in mind that you do not have to accept a deal that is not in your favor. If you do this, you would throw away all the hard work you have put into the discussion. Walking away from the negotiation is generally a preferable option to accepting a bad deal.

If you have a sufficient amount of information concerning the situation and have built up trust with your counterpart concerning the matter, another tip is to make the first offer. When you are in a negotiation, you want to have the upper hand during the process. You can do this by making the first offer to the other party. Of course, your first offer is probably not going to be accepted, but it is a good place to start and can affect how the other party will give their counteroffer.

You must be confident during the negotiation. I understand that negotiating can be a difficult process that might scare you. However, you need to portray confidence to be a good negotiator. Practice what you have to say prior to attending the negotiation so that you will feel confident. Try to look physically relaxed too because if you look tense, the other party will know that you are not confident about yourself and your offer. Try to challenge your negative thoughts prior to the conversation and banish them from your mind so that you can concentrate on the negotiation instead of getting overwhelmed.

Examples of Passive, Aggressive, and Assertive Communication

Passive	Aggressive	Assertive
Stays quiet and criticizes themselves	Talks too much and belittles other people	Expresses their needs while respecting others'
Likes to avoid eye contact and speaks in a submissive voice	Gives judgmental eye contact and speaks in a threatening voice	Maintains appropriate eye contact and talks in a relaxed voice
Avoids getting into conflicts	Always wants to be the winner in an argument	Finds a solution to solve the conflict
Allows other people to always take control	Enjoys taking control of others and situations	Expresses mutual respect between each other
Has low self-esteem	Has an arrogant personality	Has good self-esteem without being arrogant
Thinks they are less important than others	Thinks they are more important than anyone else	Thinks that no one is more important than others and believes everyone is equal
Refuses to voice their disagreements	Attacks and insults those who have different opinions	Listens to others' opinions without overlooking them

After reading these examples, what do you think your communication style is? Are you passive, aggressive, or assertive? If you are not being assertive yet, apply the skills discussed in the previous chapters to master this communication style and become a better leader for your team.

In our final chapter, we will look at steps female leaders should be taking when conflict resolution is not enough for toxic behavior in the workplace.

Dealing With Racism, Sexism, and Other Toxic Behaviors

"When a workplace becomes toxic, its poison spreads beyond its walls and into the lives of its workers and their families." – Gary Chapman

A female leader's experiences of and with discrimination need to be seen from both sides: women should not have to tolerate any form of toxic behavior, and at the same time, we have a responsibility to have zero tolerance of any behavior—from ourselves or our colleagues—that could cause discomfort for our team members.

What Are Microaggressions?

According to recent research, 61% of workers in the United States have seen or experienced workplace discrimination (Fenton, 2022). Nevertheless, it is illegal for an employer or employee to discriminate against a person based on their background identities; if this happens, legal action should be pursued. Retaliation against someone who has reported discrimination is also illegal.

There is, however, what is known as *microaggression*. Microaggressions are a more subtle type of bias towards others, whether intentional or not (Limbong, 2020). Because microaggressions may appear harmless to those who do not frequently experience discrimination, it is critical to be aware of how common and damaging they actually are. Microaggressions in the workplace can have a wide range of detrimental effects for those who experience them; these negative effects include higher levels of stress and anxiety, a decrease in job fulfillment, and a decline in the perception of justice (Ajami, 2022).

Many of us do not realize that a microaggression has occurred unless we ourselves have previously been subject to a similar form of discrimination or someone else talks about it. When someone gets called out for doing something problematic, they might act defensively and make excuses for their behavior. If another person calls us out, it is important not to try to justify our actions or words but to instead admit that we are wrong. Likewise, definitive defensive statements such as, "I'm not racist," should be avoided when taking accountability. This type of sentiment centers you in an apology that ought to be directed to others, and such all-or-nothing thinking can prevent future self-awareness, introspection, and antidiscrimination growth and learning. We should not ignore someone else's emotions, but instead learn where they are coming from. Let's take a look at some examples of microaggressions in the workplace:

- an employee being talked over and interrupted by her counterparts in meetings.

- assuming someone's gender or sexuality based on how they dress or look.

- an Asian employee being complimented for speaking

good English even though they were born in the United States.

- constantly pronouncing someone's name incorrectly because it is "too difficult"
- thinking an older colleague is unable to operate a technological device
- touching a Black colleague's hair without their consent

Other Examples of Toxic Behavior

Microaggressions are not the only toxic behavior that you can find in the workplace. There are many other examples that you might not even realize are very toxic for the work environment and culture. Toxic behavior can be carried out by the employees or management of the company and include the following:

- **Aggression:**
    - When someone is being aggressive, they can show it verbally or physically. Perhaps, you have seen a bigger coworker using their physical stature to intimidate a smaller employee. When in an argument, maybe you have witnessed someone getting shoved. Typically, the aggressor may be dealing with some personal difficulties that lead them to snap in the workplace—e.g. low self-esteem, lack of focus, resentment toward a certain colleague, or mental health issues. However, no matter how much you may empathize with someone's circumstances,

aggressiveness should never be tolerated as it is likely to escalate unless challenged. An aggressive person will hurt others and make the work environment uncomfortable and hostile.

- **Passiveness:**
  - Passive people often comply with all requests they receive and refuse to actively get into conflicts with others. I know that you might think that being passive is the way to go because all you need to do is perform your job, but being consistently passive has some strong downsides. For instance, if you were to see someone being harassed at work, when passive, you would refuse to help or call out the perpetrator, so the issue would keep going on. I know that sometimes we do not want to add more problems to our already busy lives, but being passive is not a realistic or beneficial way to approach life, especially in the workplace. For our own sake and that of others, we need to set healthy boundaries and call out inappropriate behavior before it escalates, rather than being passive.

- **Gossiping:**
  - Sometimes it's tempting to want to hear more about a juicy story circulating around the office. Curiosity is human nature. Some personal news may also help us connect and bond with our colleagues, and to a certain degree, it can even be a method of generating community safety—such as when women warn each other of the potential risks of being around an alleged sexual harasser. After all, these issues can't be address if we do not talk about them. However, this can easily devolve into toxic behavior if you gossip misinformation about people who work at the same place as you. Spreading information that

you haven't verified has a huge potential to hurt the topic of the gossip, which is something that you should never do. Moreover, gossiping will distract you from your work, and this means that it will affect your productivity negatively. Gossiping is also not good for the work environment because it can make you distrust each other and lead to conflict and stress.

- **Narcissism:**
  - A narcissistic person's major goal is to look good and get the spotlight, even at the expense of other people. Many enjoy working alone, destroying the spirits of their colleagues, and sabotaging other people's work—this is perceived to be an easier way of looking good in comparison to others, rather than putting effort into their own work. Narcissistic persons frequently lack sympathy, are entitled, and manipulate other people for their own advantage. The worst thing is that they like to take credit for other people's work whenever they have the chance.

- **Disorganization:**
  - You have likely had at least one coworker in the past who had a messy and unorganized desk; they probably often misplaced important things and were late to meetings because of that. It harms the workplace when others constantly have to wait for a person like that. What if an urgent problem needs to be solved immediately? They will cause delays that might harm the company. A disorganized person will also cause stress for other people who are likely to be handed more work last minute every time that person messes up a project.

- **Absenteeism:**

- Someone who frequently misses work is also considered very toxic. This often turns into a habit, even when they have run out of paid leave days. This will affect other employees and the company because their tasks will have to get assigned to someone else. This also can lead to the company being short-staffed and cause burnout for the employees that have to take over the tasks.

- **Pessimism:**

    - It is acceptable to complain about work from time to time. However, no one likes it if you complain too much and are pessimistic about what you have to do. When you view everything in a negative light, you are being toxic and spreading that negativity to others. People may become exhausted just from being around you because they feel demotivated by how you act and behave.

- **Sexual harassment:**

    - A toxic behavior that women have to face a lot in the workplace is sexual harassment. This involves unwanted sexual comments, offensive sexual remarks, and solicitations for sexual favors. In fact, people of all genders can experience this. Everyone can be a victim no matter what position they have in the workplace. Moreover, sexual harassment can happen verbally and physically. If you experience this, you need to go directly to management to report the perpetrator.

- **Procrastination:**

    - We all are probably guilty of procrastinating at some point in our lives. Everybody has occasional bouts of deciding to do their work later and later until the last minute. This also happens in the workplace; many employees procrastinate their work for many different reasons. Some are simply lazy and just do not do it at all. Others might also think that the work is too intimidating or difficult, so they decide to postpone it. Some are struggling with forms of neurodivergence, such as ADHD or autism, that cause severe difficulties with task initiation that are outside of their control—in these cases, workplace accommodations such as automated alarm systems or body doubling can alleviate procrastination. When someone postpones their work, they will get distracted by external forces, such as social media or a conversation with another coworker. Chronic procrastinators do not offer much in the workplace because they tend to miss deadlines or fail to complete their work.

- **Excuses:**

    - Someone is being toxic if they like to make excuses to get out of meeting their responsibilities. When they make a mistake, they will always prepare an excuse so that they do not have to face consequences. For example, if they fail to submit a task on time, they might create a sob story about their lives so that others will feel bad for them. They might have potential, but they are merely inconsistent and unreliable in their efforts. Those who like to make excuses are often not interested in the work at all and are manipulative more so than lazy.

How to Deal With Toxic Behavior in the Workplace

Working in a toxic environment is very difficult for female leaders to navigate. They have to figure out how to deal with a hostile environment while also managing their team and keeping their composure. Without realizing it, some women might also contribute to a toxic workplace environment. This is why as a female leader, you need to know how to observe and navigate your workplace while remaining willing to change your ways if you find yourself being toxic.

No one intentionally creates a toxic work environment, and often, there is no quick fix that you can use when you notice that toxicity has seeped in. When a leader fails to establish rules to punish those with toxic behaviors, their work culture will suffer. As a leader, you need to raise your awareness level and start observing what is going on around you. You must take steps to resolve a toxic environment so that your team can work better.

Let's explore how you can navigate the toxic culture within your team: The first step you need to take is to define what kind of leader you wish to be for your team members. You should concentrate on your strengths and work with them to address potential pitfalls. If there are some habits you would like to change, you can start with one behavior at a time. Make a commitment to be better, and start with small but steady steps. Perhaps, you could ask another person, like a mentor, for assistance.

It is also vital to become more self-aware and observe how you may be creating a toxic environment. If you find yourself being toxic, you should not overlook your behavior. You must admit your mistake so that you can make changes. Additionally, it is important to create a supportive environment by setting good examples, being open and honest, delegating tasks, and acknowledging your team's hard work.

Furthermore, it is also important to know how to navigate a toxic culture outside of your team. You can initially approach this by observing the social interactions in your workplace. How do you feel about them? Are they positive or negative? You need to be honest about how they are and understand how they impact you. Do you feel safe in your workplace? If not, you may need to leave. Do not tolerate it! I understand that it will be hard. We must speak up and voice our concerns when something toxic happens. We all have our limits, and this is why you must set your own boundaries and learn how to say no to people. As a leader, you can find friends and allies who want to support each other in the workplace. The most important thing is to educate yourself more. When you are informed, you will be better at navigating toxic culture and encouraging others to become more positive.

Creating a Positive Workplace Culture

We all know that women these days have more opportunities than ever. However, that doesn't mean that we live and work in a utopia free from discrimination. There are still so many things to improve to provide an equitable employment experience for women. The good thing is that it is possible to create more changes as we go along. Professionals of all genders can work together to establish an inclusive workplace so that women can flourish and advance their careers. The following are some approaches to consider in creating this change:

- **Improving flexibility:**

- When employees are given flexible work hours and the chance to work from home, their productivity and motivation levels will also rise. As a result, the company will become more profitable and the employees will be happier in the workplace. Flexible hours allow skilled women to enter the workforce without having to choose between their personal and professional lives.

- **Taking the initiative to promote equality:**
    - As a leader, you have the power to influence the environment in the workplace. You can use your voice to provide a good example for your employees. When a leader does something, it signals that the action is appropriate and others follow them.

- **Prioritizing skills rather than qualifications:**
    - Many of us think a person is suitable for a job because of the qualifications on their resume. It is now up to you to change that belief and focus on skills instead. This will allow women to have an equal opportunity in the hiring process. Many women and people from minority groups struggle to have access to educational and professional achievements and qualifications. This means that their resume might not look so promising for recruiters. If you only focus on their qualifications, you will only hire privileged people.

- **Removing unconscious bias in the hiring process:**
    - Women still experience a variety of biases when they apply for a job, especially if it's a role that is perceived to be masculine. One hiring technique to potentially incorporate is what we call "blind hiring," where someone's name, gender identity, and other personal identifiers are hidden from their ap-

plication during the screening process so that they can have an equal opportunity to be accepted for the position.

- **Implementing a zero-tolerance policy:**
    - Nowadays, we have seen many instances where leaders are exposed for their inappropriate behavior in the workplace. As a leader, you need to call out and give consequences to those who harass other people. Women deserve to feel safe in their workplace. This is why you should implement a zero-tolerance policy for harassment that everyone must adhere to.

- **Taking accountability:**
    - We can create change if we take accountability. Oftentimes, discrimination happens because we have prejudices against groups of people. If you ever find yourself acting from a place of ignorance or bias, you need to hold yourself accountable and admit your mistakes so that you can change your mindset. To encourage inclusivity and foster a supportive work environment, we must start by changing how we behave and act first.

Let's take a look at an example of how someone was bullied out of their job and found success afterward: Jane was always a diligent employee and worked outside of regular office hours to complete a project, even when no one told her so. Then, there was a project with a difficult client that nobody could please; Jane was asked to take over. She had to work over 12 hours a day for weeks just to make the client happy. When the project finally ended and the client was satisfied, her CEO only said, "It would have been better if you could finish it sooner." It was so unprofessional and passive-aggressive. Jane then realized how her work ethic was under-appreciated and taken advantage of from the start, and it became her breaking point. She decided to vent to a colleague about her situation, who fortunately worked at a startup that was expanding and would need new members soon. With that internal referral and a few positive interviews, Jane was able to begin a similar role within a few months at her colleague's company with a much healthier work-life balance and a salary increase for her expertise.

Toxic Work Culture Checklist

It is difficult to work and try to be productive in a toxic workplace. This is why you need to maintain a level of observation that enables you to see toxicity building. Here is a checklist of toxic behaviors that commonly happen in the workplace so that you can notice and work to resolve them. Check in with this list and reevaluate your workplace every 8–12 weeks to ensure that patterns of toxic behavior can be challenged before becoming habitual aspects of your workplace environment.

Toxic Behaviors	Checklist
Rumors and gossip	
Intimidation, harassment, and bullying	
Pessimistic behavior	
Lack of communication	
Procrastination and laziness	
Disorganization	
Dictatorship	
Unreliable or dishonest business activities	
Frequent absenteeism	
Excessive overtime	

If you notice these behaviors becoming prevalent in your workplace, taking an assertive stance and utilizing the communication skills described throughout this book can help you to challenge these patterns and create a better environment for everyone you work with.

Conclusion

We have reached the end of this book at last. How do you feel? Are you satisfied with yourself? I, personally, would like to congratulate you on finishing this first step on your journey to becoming a more effective communicator! This book has provided you with suggestions and insights on how to become a better leader by expressing and voicing your opinions. It is now the time for you to take action and use all the tools given to you. Theory can only get you so far; it's time to put it into practice to become a great female leader.

The book has taught you various things about communication skills. Let's review some of them: As a leader, it is crucial to know how to use positive body language when interacting with people so that they feel respected and valued. It is also important to actively listen when speaking to someone so that you receive the intended message and respond accordingly. Active listening helps you stay focused and process information without outside distractions.

Moreover, you must know how to show empathy. By empathizing with others, you show that you care about their feelings. With no empathy, you become a cold leader whose team members will struggle without asking for or feeling able to accept support. In this technological era, you also need reliable written and digital communication skills so that you may send emails or video call your team easily when you have to interact through the internet.

Most importantly, a leader must be assertive. Being assertive will convince people to listen to you and be collaborative while also demonstrating that you care about their needs and feelings. As you can see, communication skills are very essential for your team building and career advancement.

It is true that there are still far too many biases and stereotypes in the workplace, but we are in the middle of a revolution of social change. It is normal to get frustrated, but the only way we can continue what our previous generations started is to actively stand up and say no: no to gender pay inequality, no to women of color not having the same freedom to advance, and no to the unfair distribution of opportunities. It has been proven time and time again that women make phenomenal leaders. We just need to find our voices and speak up.

In 2019, only 15% of CEOs and managing directors were female, but this increased to 26% by 2021 (*Women in Management*, 2022). The fight is slow, but we are making changes. Your success story can be part of this change, and imagine the difference you could make for the next generation. You know what you need to do! Take a pen and paper, grab yourself your favorite drink, and make a list of what needs to be done in your workplace.

I love hearing how women are finding their places, their voices, and being who they are meant to be. Sharing your review gives me a chance to learn about these stories and continue to provide valuable content. However, your reviews mean more than this. Your opinion could reach another woman and provide her with the confidence and skills she needs to be a part of this much-needed change. So, please be sure to review this book if you have found it helpful, and good luck with your onward communication journey.

References

Agarwal, P. (2018, December 17). *Here is how unconscious bias holds women back*. Forbes. https://www.forbes.com/sites/pragyaagarwaleurope/2018/12/17/here-is-how-unconscious-bias-holds-women-back/?sh=3240b6b32d4f

Ajami, L. (2022, April 14). *7 examples of workplace microaggressions and how to steer clear*. Berlitz. https://www.berlitz.com/blog/examples-microaggressions-workplace

Anderson, K. (2023, February 3). *8 strategies to improve your listening skills*. Indeed. https://www.indeed.com/career-advice/career-development/how-to-be-a-good-listener

Aragao, C. (2023, March 1). *Gender pay gap in the U.S. hasn't changed much in two years*. Pew Research Center. https://www.pewresearch.org/short-reads/2023/03/01/gender-pay-gap-facts/#:~:text=The%20gender%20gap%20in%20pay,%2D%20and%20part%2Dtime%20workers.

Ariella, S. (2022, November 9). *25 women in leadership statistics [2023]: facts on the gender gap in corporate and political leadership*. Zippia. https://www.zippia.com/advice/women-in-leadership-statistics/

Arnold, C. (n.d.). *How to start a women's networking group at work*. The EW Group. https://theewgroup.com/blog/womens-network-guide/

Arora, A. (2017, July 17). *What is paralanguage?* Visme. https://visme.co/blog/what-is-paralanguage/

Badgujar, V. (2023). *10 common toxic workplace behaviors and how to prevent them*. Time Doctor. https://www.timedoctor.com/blog/toxic-workplace-behaviors/
Baker, C. (2022, June 20). *Master active listening with these 11 techniques*. Leaders. https://leaders.com/articles/leadership/active-listening/
Bansal, V. (2021). *Body language in the workplace: Art of effective communication*. Tech Tello. https://www.techtello.com/body-language-in-the-workplace/
The binary choice for leadership. (2023). Archimedes Speaks. https://archimedesspeaks.com/women/strong-or-compassionate-leadership-why-not-both
Botwin, A. (2022, January 17). *7 challenges female leaders face in the workplace and how to combat them*. Strategy People Culture. https://www.strategypeopleculture.com/blog/challenges-female-leaders-face-in-the-workplace/
Buffalmano, L. (n.d.). *The 4 communication styles: Description and examples*. The Power Moves. https://thepowermoves.com/communication-styles/
Burlinson, K. (2021, April 13). *Confidence tips: 8 ways for women to take up space in online meetings*. Future Talent Learning. https://www.futuretalentlearning.com/en/future-talent-learning-blog/confidence-tips-8-ways-for-women-to-take-up-space-in-online-meetings
Business networking quotes. (2023). Quotes Gram. https://quotesgram.com/business-networking-quotes/
Cain, M. (2011, October 13). *Don't take this personally, but you take things personally*. Forbes. https://www.forbes.com/sites/glassheel/2011/10/13/dont-take-this-personally-but-you-take-things-too-personally/?sh=46d7432c5a75
Calero-Holmes, B. (2023, February 22). *10 negotiating tips to sharpen your skills*. Business News Daily. https://www.businessnewsdaily.com/7349-negotiating-donts.html

Can Empathic Leadership be the Secret to Your Success on a Team? (2021, September 24). Rock Content. https://rockcontent.com/blog/empathic-leadership/

Cartwright, J. (2022, April 21). *Stuff they don't tell you – how to survive a toxic workplace.* We Present. https://wepresent.wetransfer.com/stories/stuff-they-dont-tell-you-toxic-workplace

Cherry, K. (2023, February 23). *Understanding body language and facial expressions.* Very Well Mind. https://www.verywellmind.com/understand-body-language-and-facial-expressions-4147228

Colby, S. (2023, May 16). *What are filler words? 11 super common words.* Resound. https://www.resound.fm/blog/what-are-filler-words

Communication styles. (2023). Pumble. https://pumble.com/learn/communication/communication-styles/

Communication styles. (2023, February 14). Valamis. https://www.valamis.com/hub/communication-styles

Conflict resolution strategies for inclusive leaders. (2021, August 4). St. Catherine University. https://www.stkate.edu/academics/women-in-leadership-degrees/conflict-resolution-strategies

Connley, C. (2022, November 23). *The real reason why women and people of color receive less feedback at work.* Chief. https://chief.com/articles/feedback-style

Conversation starters – do's and don'ts. (2021, March 24). ASAP. https://www.asaporg.com/communication/conversation-starters-dos-and-don-ts

Cooks-Campbell, A. (2022, August 1). *How to negotiate: 7 tips for effective negotiation.* Better Up. https://www.betterup.com/blog/how-to-negotiate

Corbin-Herbison, C. (2019, September 13). *Pros and cons of digital workplace – striking a human balance.* Interact Software. https://www.interactsoftware.com/blog/pros-cons-digital-workplace/

REFERENCES 133

Cuncic, A. (2022, November 9). *What is active listening?* Very Well Mind. https://www.verywellmind.com/what-is-active-listening-3024343

Dahl, D. (2023, February 26). *50 women supporting women quotes to spread positivity*. Everyday Power. https://everydaypower.com/women-supporting-women-quotes/

Datta, S. (n.d.). *7 micro expressions for understanding body language*. Sanjeev Datta. https://sanjeevdatta.com/7-micro-expressions/

Discovering the glass cliff: Insights into addressing subtle gender discrimination in the workplace. (2023). University of Exeter. https://psychology.exeter.ac.uk/cic/about/theglasscliff/#a0

Eatough, E. (2021, September 9). *Eye contact is important (crucial really) in communication.* Better Up. https://www.betterup.com/blog/why-is-eye-contact-important

Edwards, V. (2016, November 17). *The definitive guide to reading microexpressions*. Medium. https://medium.com/@vvanedwards/how-to-decode-the-7-basic-emotions-140561f2ccdf

Edwards, V. (2023). *Decoding vocals – 21 cues of paralanguage & prosody to know.* Science of People. https://www.scienceofpeople.com/paralanguage/

Evans, C. (2020, October 20). *The benefits of active listening.* LinkedIn. https://www.linkedin.com/pulse/benefits-active-listening-carey-evans/

Exploring the 3 main ways that emotional intelligence will improve your communication in the workplace. (2022). In Professional Development. https://www.inpd.co.uk/blog/3-ways-emotional-intelligence-will-improve-your-communication#:~:text=Emotional%20Intelligence%20can%20improve%20your,calm%2C%20professional%20and%20clear%20manner.

Felix, A. (2018, October 1). *Telling Elizabeth Warren's story.* Minnesota Women's Press. https://www.womenspress.com/telling-elizabeth-warrens-story/

Fenton, M. K. (2022, July 18). *2022 employment discrimination statistics employees need to know*. Wenzel Fenton. https://www.wenzelfenton.com/blog/2022/07/18/employment-discrimination-statistics-employees-need-to-know/

15 key steps leaders can take to prepare for an important stakeholder meeting. (2021, October 14). Forbes. https://www.forbes.com/sites/forbescoachescouncil/2021/10/14/15-key-steps-leaders-can-take-to-prepare-for-an-important-stakeholder-meeting/?sh=6b0a06de69b2

15 quotes about self-love for strong women to remember. (2023, May 21). Power of Positivity. https://www.powerofpositivity.com/quotes-about-self-love-strong-women/

5 major communication problems women in the workplace face – and how to overcome them. (2023). Zencare. https://blog.zencare.co/communication-problems-work/

Five ways women can negotiate more effectively. (n.d.). Kellogg Insight. https://insight.kellogg.northwestern.edu/article/five-ways-women-can-negotiate-more-effectively

Fleishman, H. (2022, November 9). *How to network effectively: 15 tips you can start using today*. Hub Spot. https://blog.hubspot.com/marketing/the-ultimate-guide-to-non_awkward-effective-networking

4 Advantages of an empathetic leadership style. (2022, August 31). Australian Institute of Business. https://www.aib.edu.au/blog/leadership/4-advantages-of-an-empathetic-leadership-style/

Galli, E. (2022). *Toxic work environment: Diagnosis and treatment*. Starred. https://www.starred.com/blog/toxic-work-environments

Garcia, M. (2021, June 9). *The importance of facial expressions in the workplace*. Medium. https://marygarcia455151.medium.com/the-importance-of-facial-expression-in-the-workplace-656285677442

Gatchpazian, A. (n.d.). *Assertive communication: Definition, examples, & techniques*. Berkeley Well-Being. https://www.berkeleywellbeing.com/assertive-communication.html

Gebel, M. (2023, April 18). *Why you need sponsors (not just mentors)—and how to find them*. The Muse. https://www.themuse.com/advice/sponsor-vs-mentor

Gillham, R. (2022, November 3). *How To Improve Written Communication Skills At Work (8 Tips To Follow)*. Blinkist. https://www.blinkist.com/magazine/posts/how-to-improve-written-communication-skills-at-work

Goman, C. (2022). *To read body language like a pro, look for clusters*. Vunela. https://www.vunela.com/to-read-body-language-like-a-pro-look-for-clusters/

Helen Fisher's quotes. (n.d.). Quote Fancy. https://quotefancy.com/quote/1532647/Helen-Fisher-Women-are-better-at-reading-body-language-everywhere-in-the-world-As-a

Herrity, J. (2022, September 30). *150 helpful conversation starters for networking professionals*. Indeed. https://www.indeed.com/career-advice/career-development/work-conversation-starters

Herrity, J. (2023, February 3). *4 types of communication styles and how to improve yours*. Indeed. https://www.indeed.com/career-advice/career-development/communication-styles

How can I overcome communication barriers? (2020, February 24). NSW Health. https://www.health.nsw.gov.au/mentalhealth/psychosocial/strategies/Pages/communicating-barriers.aspx

How much of communication is nonverbal? (2023). The University of Texas Permian Basin. https://online.utpb.edu/about-us/articles/communication/how-much-of-communication-is-nonverbal/

How to give and receive feedback: Keys for leaders. (2022, February 22). IESE Business School. https://www.iese.edu/standout/feedback-give-receive-keys/

How to politely end a conversation at a networking event. (n.d.). US Veteran Magazine. https://usveteransmagazine.com/2017/10/politely-end-conversation-networking-event/

How to prepare for a presentation, with examples. (2023). Virtual Speech. https://virtualspeech.com/blog/how-to-prepare-for-a-presentation

How Women Leaders Overcome Conflicting Expectations. (n.d.). Ideas for Leaders. https://ideasforleaders.com/Ideas/how-women-leaders-overcome-conflicting-expectations/

Ibarra, H. (2019, August 19). *A lack of sponsorship is keeping women from advancing into leadership.* Harvard Business Review. https://hbr.org/2019/08/a-lack-of-sponsorship-is-keeping-women-from-advancing-into-leadership

Importance of gestures in public speaking. (2018, March 21). Medium. https://the-stage.medium.com/importance-of-gestures-in-public-speaking-3ece0d692921

Increasing the representation of minority ethnic women in management and leadership. (2022, March 8). University of Birmingham. https://blog.bham.ac.uk/business-school/2022/03/08/bame-leadership/

Johansson, A. (2019, March 20). *How women can be more assertive in the workplace.* Witi. https://witi.com/articles/1550/How-Women-Can-Be-More-Assertive-in-the-Workplace/

Kagan, J. (2022, December 7). *Glass cliff: Definition, research, examples, vs. glass ceiling.* Investopedia. https://www.investopedia.com/terms/g/glass-cliff.asp

Karabell, S. (2016, January 16). *Dressing like a leader: Style tips for women in the spotlight.* Forbes. https://www.forbes.com/sites/shelliekarabell/2016/01/16/dressing-like-a-leader-style-tips-for-women-in-the-spotlight/?sh=4c06520f2466

Kashyap, S. (2023). *How to choose a project management software: A complete guide.* Proof Hub. https://www.proofhub.com/articles/choosing-a-project-management-software/

Keiling, H. (2023, February 4). *9 types of nonverbal communication and how to understand them.* Indeed. https://www.indeed.com/career-advice/career-development/nonverbal-communication-skills#:~:text=1.-,Posture,be%20nervous%2C%20anxious%20or%20angry.

REFERENCES

Khazan, O. (2013, December 2). *Male and female brains are really built differently*. The Atlantic. https://www.theatlantic.com/health/archive/2013/12/male-and-female-brains-really-are-built-differently/281962/

King, M. P. (2021, October 26). *The authority gap: Why women are still taken less seriously than men*. Forbes. https://www.forbes.com/sites/michelleking/2021/10/26/the-authority-gap-why-women-are-still-taken-less-seriously-than-men/?sh=58471cef634d

Klimuk, E. (2022, May 30). *What are the benefits of active listening?* Support Bench. https://www.supportbench.com/what-are-the-benefits-of-active-listening/

LaMantina, B. & Ma, J. (2022, February 2). *25 famous female leaders in power*. The Cut. https://www.thecut.com/article/25-famous-female-leaders-on-empowerment.html

Lestari, T., Setyowati, A., & Yukesti, T. (2019). Gender-based violence against the female main character in Colleen Hoover's It Ends With Us. *Journal of English Literature, language, and Culture, 1*(2), 102-115.

Limbong, A. (2020, June 9). *Microaggressions are a big deal: How to talk them out and when to walk away*. NPR. https://www.npr.org/2020/06/08/872371063/microaggressions-are-a-big-deal-how-to-talk-them-out-and-when-to-walk-away

Manning, T. (2021, November 22). *Overcoming the biggest challenges for women in leadership: communicating clearly and effectively on a male dominated team*. Tricia Manning. https://triciamanning.com/overcoming-the-biggest-challenges-for-women-in-leadership-communicating-clearly-and-effectively-on-a-male-dominated-team/

Manning, T. (2021, September 28). *How to delegate with intention: A key skill for women in business leadership*. LinkedIn. https://www.linkedin.com/pulse/how-delegate-intention-key-skill-women-business-tricia-manning/

Martins, J. (2022, June 15). *The 4 communication styles every manager should know.* Asana. https://asana.com/resources/communication-styles

Microexpressions: A universal language you wear on your face. (2020, April 29). Orlando Science Center. https://www.osc.org/microexpressions-universal-language/#:~:text=He%20traveled%20the%20world%20studying,After%20even%20more%20study%2C%20Dr.

Nordquist, R. (2019, May 24). *Intonation definition and examples in speech.* ThoughtCo. https://www.thoughtco.com/intonation-speech-term-1691184

Nwanne, E. (2021, August 20). *The 5 communication styles and how to use them effectively.* Charma. https://www.charma.com/resources/communication-styles

Peek, S. (2023, February 22). *Want to be a good leader? Step 1: Know thyself.* Business News Daily. https://www.businessnewsdaily.com/6097-self-awareness-in-leadership.html

Perez, M. J. (2022, July 25). *How women leaders navigate toxic workplaces.* LinkedIn. https://www.linkedin.com/pulse/how-women-leaders-navigate-toxic-workplaces-mari-j-perez-pcc/?trk=pulse-article_more-articles_related-content-card

Prohibited employment policies/practices. (2023). U.S. Equal Employment Opportunity Commission. https://www.eeoc.gov/prohibited-employment-policiespractices

Rhymes, S. (2023). *7 ways to make better, more confident eye contact.* In Her Sight. https://www.inhersight.com/blog/career-development/eye-contact

Saulsbery, A. (2023). *Contempt: Definition, causes, and examples.* Berkeley Well-Being. https://www.berkeleywellbeing.com/contempt.html

Segal, J., Smith, M., Robinson, L., & Boose, G. (2023). *Nonverbal communication and body language.* Help Guide. https://www.helpguide.org/articles/relationships-communication/nonverbal-communication.htm

7 ways to improve workplace equality. (2023). Energy Resourcing. https://energyresourcing.com/blog/build-workplace-where-women-thrive

74 technology quotes to inspire innovation. (2023, January 30). Gracious Quotes. https://graciousquotes.com/technology/

Soholowsky, J. (2023). *What are workplace sponsorship programs?* Chronus. https://chronus.com/blog/what-are-workplace-sponsorship-programs

Stanborough, R. (2019, June 29). *Smiling with your eyes: What exactly is a Duchenne Smile?* Healthline. https://www.healthline.com/health/duchenne-smile

Stress management. (2022, May 13). Mayo Clinic. https://www.mayoclinic.org/healthy-lifestyle/stress-management/in-depth/assertive/art-20044644

The successful woman's guide to setting boundaries – without being a bitch. (2016). Women Igniting Change. https://womenignitingchange.com/blog/the-successful-womans-guide-to-setting-boundaries-without-being-a/

Swami, S. (2010, October 30). *Women are body language experts.* The Scientific Portal of Behavior, Body Language and Nonverbal Communication. http://www.nonverbal-world.com/2010/10/women-are-body-language-experts.html

Swami, S. (2022, February 1). *Reading body language – baseline.* The Scientific Portal of Behavior, Body Language and Nonverbal Communication. http://www.nonverbal-world.com/2022/02/reading-body-language-baseline.html

Taylor, P. (n,d.). *Importance of the baseline in body language.* Body Language Matters. https://bodylanguagematters.com/importance-of-the-baseline-in-body-language/

10 signs of a toxic workplace: A checklist for managers. (n.d.). HIS. https://hsi.com/blog/10-signs-of-a-toxic-workplace-a-checklist-for-managers

10 tips for active listening. (2023). British Heart Foundation. https://www.bhf.org.uk/informationsupport/heart-matters

-magazine/wellbeing/how-to-talk-about-health-problems/active-listening

The Female Lead [@the_female_lead]. (2020, July 28). *To the women who are labelled bossy, keep leading. To the women who are labeled aggressive, keep being assertive. To the women who are labeled difficult, keep telling the truth. Gender bias is real and the language we use is important* [Tweet]. Twitter. https://twitter.com/the_female_lead/status/1288112036644175879

How good are your communication skills? (2023). Mind Tools. https://www.mindtools.com/a3y5cte/how-good-are-your-communication-skills

These are the absolute best places to network. (2018, March 24). Job Monkey. https://www.jobmonkey.com/best-places-to-network/

Thompson, J. (2011, September 30*). Is nonverbal communication a numbers game?* Psychology Today. https://www.psychologytoday.com/us/blog/beyond-words/201109/is-nonverbal-communication-numbers-game

Tran, K. (2018, August 15). *Communication problems in the digital workplace.* Teg International. https://blog.trginternational.com/communication-problems-in-the-digital-workplace

Understanding context. (2023). Improve Your Social Skills. https://www.improveyoursocialskills.com/body-language/understanding-context

Understanding violence and sexual harassment. (2023). Our Watch. https://workplace.ourwatch.org.au/understanding-violence-and-sexual-harassment/

Valenzuela, D. (2022, September 23). *Do men and women actually communicate differently? Experts weigh in.* Katie Couric Media. https://katiecouric.com/lifestyle/relationships/gender-differences-in-communication-style/#:~:text=patterns%20of%20communication%3F-,Dr.,when%20women%20communicate%20with%20others.

REFERENCES

Voris, B. (2020, March 11). *How women can find mentors?* Berkeley Haas. https://blogs.haas.berkeley.edu/the-berkeley-mba/how-women-can-find-mentors

Waters, S. (2021, June 7). *How to become more assertive at work (your ultimate guide)*. Better Up. https://www.betterup.com/blog/assertiveness

What do employers mean by 'excellent communication skills'? (2018). Ambition. https://www.ambition.co.uk/blog/2017/06/what-do-employers-mean-by-excellent-communication-skills

What is an empathetic leader? (Plus tips on how to become one). (2023, February 3). Indeed. https://www.indeed.com/career-advice/career-development/empathetic-leaders

Why empathy & emotional intelligence are key leadership skills. (2022, May 6). Piper. https://www.piperhq.co/resources/why-empathy-emotional-intelligence-are-key-leadership-skills

Why is body language important in communication? (2023). John Academy. https://www.johnacademy.co.uk/why-is-body-language-important-in-communication/

Women in management. (2022, March 1). Catalyst. https://www.catalyst.org/research/women-in-management/

Wooll, M. (2021, September 23). *Mentor vs. sponsor: Why having both is key for your career*. Better Up. https://www.betterup.com/blog/mentor-vs-sponsor

Zenger, J. & Folkman, J. (2019, June 25). *Research: Women score higher than men in most leadership skills*. Harvard Business Review. https://hbr.org/2019/06/research-women-score-higher-than-men-in-most-leadership-skills

Zhao, S. & Smith, R. (2023). *6 barriers for women's career advancement*. People Matters. https://www.peoplematters.in/article/diversity/6-barriers-womens-career-advancement-12645

Acknowledgements

Kyrabe Stories was founded by Kyndall Bennett, a veteran passionate about education and leadership. Her experiences in the US Navy have given her a deep insight into women's struggles in a male-dominated workforce. Through her career exploration journey into the eLearning industry, she realized a need for a safe, educational place to provide professional development resources and relatable stories to those who desired a change in their lives but weren't sure where to begin.

With such an overwhelming response to Kyrabe Stories, Kyndall collaborated with the Publishing Services research team along with the writing and editing professionals, Widhi Way and AJ Kearney, to construct the content within this book. Kyndall is striving to help more women improve their personal and professional development, unleash their confidence, and advance the necessary skills they need for leadership.

To explore additional resources, you can visit the Kyrabe Stories blog at KyrabeStories.com or connect with Kyndall Bennett on LinkedIn: LinkedIn.com/in/KyndallBennett

Follow Kyrabe Stories on social media:
- Twitter: @KyrabeStories

- Facebook: @KyrabeStories

- TikTok: @KyrabeStories
- Instagram: @KyrabeStories

Printed in Great Britain
by Amazon